CREATING A CRIME-FREE SOCIETY THROUGH PROPER FAMILY VALUES

Gbenga Anola

Greenvine Diamond Resources

ISBN 979-8-9927916-0-0

Published by
Greenvine Diamond Resources

Made in USA
Wichitafalls, Texas
12 March 2025

Cover Design and formatting by Dkgrafix
(dkenterpriseglobal@gmail.com or +234 703 755 4987)

For enquiries, contact: worldcrimefree@gmail.com

CONTENTS

ACKNOWLEDGEMENT

I extend my heartfelt gratitude to God for inspiring me to write this book, with the aim of bringing about a positive change in our society.

I am deeply appreciative of my wife, Faith Anola, and my children, Mary, Testimony, and Peter, for their unwavering support and sacrifices that made it possible for me to complete this work.

I also express my sincere gratitude to my late father, Joseph Anola, my mother, Julianah Anola, and my mother-in-law, Elizabeth Uwaya, for their profound influence and support in my life.

INTRODUCTION

It is general knowledge that the primary platforms that impart societal norms are the home and the schools, meaning that a dysfunction in any of these platforms will impact negatively on the society. In my several years of work in correctional facilities, I have encountered many inmates who attribute their involvement in crime to early family separation or parental abandonment—in most stories, somehow, somewhere, it all comes down to some sort of family dysfunction. I once encountered an inmate during my work as a correctional officer. While searching his cell, I noticed a few thought-provoking inscriptions on the wall, such as *"You can create your world by your words"* and *"Be good to yourself by being nice to people."* After completing the search and returning him to his cell, I asked who had written those words. He replied, *"I did."*

He went on to tell me how his father had tried to raise him well, but *he chose not to listen.* When I asked about his mother, he explained that his parents had separated when he was very young. Reflecting on his situation, I couldn't help but wonder—if both parents had stayed and worked together to guide and train him, perhaps he wouldn't have ended up in prison. Something may have cracked within him due to their separation, preventing his father's efforts from yielding the expected results.

Moreover, when you examine the prison population, a significant percentage of inmates come from divorced or separated homes. This realization formed the foundation and motivation for me to write this.

The institution of marriage, primarily made up of parents, plays a significant role in the socialization of children and in shaping the broader environment in which they grow. Marriage, as an institution, has the power to influence the behaviors of individuals by assigning them specific roles—whether positive or negative—that are often absorbed by children. The impact of this institution on the psychological well-being of children should not be underestimated, as the psychological state of a child is crucial to their overall performance, especially in the educational system. The way children are raised and the homes they come from serve as a foundational training ground, influencing their development from birth through their schooling years.

It is essential to recognize that while the family cannot take the sole blame for crime in society, the role of family dynamics—including disruptions such as separation or divorce—cannot also be overlooked. Crime is a complex social phenomenon influenced by numerous factors, including economic conditions, environmental influences, cultural norms, and individual experiences. However, family disruptions, such as divorce or separation, can create emotional stress, financial strain, and a lack of support, which may affect an individual's mental health and behavior, potentially leading to criminal activity if not properly addressed.

This book does not also aim to generalize that all individuals from separated families engage in criminal behavior, as many factors contribute to criminal activity such as socio-economic conditions, education, and emotional states. Systemic issues like poverty, inequality, and limited access to resources also encourage crime. Nonetheless, this discussion does not diminish the importance of examining the family's role in facilitating criminal behavior, especially since family dynamics can contribute to or exacerbate other factors that lead to crime in society.

Through my work in correctional facilities, I have encountered many inmates who attribute their involvement in crime to early family separation or parental abandonment. Many claim that they turned to crime, such as joining drug cartels, because their fathers left them at a critical stage in their lives, often just before high school graduation, leaving them without the necessary guidance and resources. Family may not be the sole cause of crime, but it can be seen as a leading factor, particularly in cases of divorce or separation, where emotional, mental, and social instability can lead to criminal behavior. Studies show that a significant percentage of teenagers who engage in drug use come from divorced households. The age at which the parents divorced is directly linked to the likelihood of drug use in teens, with those experiencing parental separation at an earlier age being more vulnerable.

While government efforts to increase law enforcement and security are important, it is equally crucial to address the root causes of insecurity in society, particularly the role of family in shaping a child's values and behavior. Children need strong parenting to navigate life's challenges, peer pressure, and social learning. The transformative power of the home cannot therefore be overstated. Teachers and school officials have long recognized that a child's behavior, academic performance, and interactions with peers are heavily influenced by their home life. A strong partnership between the home and school is therefore essential for raising well-rounded individuals. Unfortunately, too little focus is placed on improving the role of the family in nurturing a child's growth. Governments often focus more on holding parents accountable for their mistakes than ensuring the overall well-being of children. For vulnerable children, the primary concern should be their safety and security, especially considering the prevalence of crime and the rise in broken homes.

Children from broken families often suffer untold psychological trauma that lingers long after the event. Often happening at a stage in life when they have little understanding of how to cope with such challenges, these children may struggle emotionally, leading them to seek unhealthy ways of coping, including criminal behavior. Without proper mentoring or guidance, these children may fall into deviant behavior.

To address these challenges, society must invest in readily accessible psychological support for children, identifying and addressing the psychological trauma they may face. Mentoring, or looking after one another, should be emphasized as a vital means of preserving values and preventing deviant behavior. Mentoring involves the steady transfer of knowledge and support over time, helping to guide children through difficult situations and shaping their decisions in a positive direction.

Maybe you've been wondering what may have inspired this great book. Well, three key factors: my profession as a correctional officer, my academic exposure through a Master of Arts in Criminal Justice, and society's collective yearning to be free from crime. These pillars form the basis of this book, which is highly recommended for parents and families in the United States and around the world.

GBENGA ANOLA

CHAPTER 1: WHY WE NEED TO BUILD A NEW SOCIETY THROUGH FAMILY

Security concerns have become a global issue affecting people in various locations, such as schools, grocery stores, restaurants, churches, mosques, event centers, and other public spaces. People everywhere are increasingly anxious about their safety, given the rise of crime and violence. Modern technologies have been developed to address these security challenges, including tools like metal detectors, tracking devices, and electronic surveillance equipment, all of which are used by law enforcement to track and combat crime.

The United States, as revealed in a study, accounted for

67 percent of all mass shootings in developed countries between 1998 and 2019. One of the most devastating incidents occurred when Adam Lanza, the active shooter responsible for the Sandy Hook Elementary School tragedy in December 2012, killed 26 people, including 20 children aged six and seven. Lanza, who had a strained relationship with his divorced parents and suffered from mental health issues, fatally shot his mother before carrying out the massacre. His tragic actions serve as a stark example of how family disruptions, such as divorce, can contribute to emotional distress and violent behavior.

Another example is Nickolas Cruz, the Parkland high school shooter, who killed 17 people and injured 17 others in a mass shooting at Marjory Stoneman Douglas High School in February 2018. Cruz, whose adoptive parents had both died, had a troubled upbringing marked by behavioral problems and emotional instability.

Similarly, the tragic shooting at Robb Elementary School in Uvalde, Texas, where 21 people were killed, including Irma Garcia and Eva Mireles, highlights the devastating consequences of gun violence. Garcia's husband, Joe, died from a heart attack just days after learning of his wife's death.

Even former President Donald Trump was not immune to violence, as he survived two assassination attempts —one at a rally in Butler, Pennsylvania, and another at his Florida golf course. These incidents highlight the vulnerability of even the most prominent individuals to acts of violence.

Dylann Roof's radicalization online and the mass shooting he committed at the Charleston church in 2015 is a further example of how family instability, coupled with external influences like online hate, can lead to tragic outcomes. Roof's parents were divorced, and his chaotic upbringing contributed to his violent behavior. Elliot Rodger, responsible for a mass killing in Isla Vista, California, in 2014, similarly had a troubled childhood, marked by mental health issues and parental separation. His actions underscore the importance of providing support for children facing emotional and psychological struggles, as these issues can escalate into violent behavior if left unaddressed.

Other mass shootings, such as the one during the Independence Day celebration in Highland Park, Chicago, and a similar incident in Philadelphia, exemplify how public events can become sites of terror. The fear and uncertainty caused by such violence have led many people to reconsider attending public gatherings, as the risk of being caught in a shooting becomes an ever-present concern.

In addition to the United States, similar shootings have occurred globally, such as the mass shooting at the Kurdish Cultural Center in Paris, which resulted in three deaths.

Despite the introduction of new laws and advanced security technologies, insecurity continues to persist, affecting people of all backgrounds, regardless of their social or economic status.

Back To The Foundations

This ongoing threat to safety underscores the need to go back to the foundations, instead of merely treating symptoms.

First is the need to make God the foundation of our security system. As Psalm 127:1 reminds us—*"Unless the Lord builds the house, they labor in vain who build it; unless the Lord guards the city, the watchman stays awake in vain."* It is important to note that this Scripture does not abdicate every responsibility from man; it simply emphasizes the need to make sure that God is at the very foundation of the efforts of the laborer and the watchman. Therefore, our faith in God's ability to protect us should be coupled with practical measures to safeguard our well-being. Just as Jesus instructed those around Lazarus to remove the stone from his tomb before performing the miracle, we must take action and use the tools available to us, while trusting in God's protection. Faith, coupled with works, is the mix essential to securing both our physical and spiritual well-being.

Secondly, the ongoing threat to safety also underscores the need to restrategize and put more attention to the family. Building a new society begins with the foundation of strong, healthy families.

Why The Family?

The family unit is the cornerstone of any society, as it shapes the values, beliefs, and behaviors of future generations. A thriving family environment is essential for creating individuals who contribute positively to the community and society at large. By fostering love, respect, responsibility, and support within families, we cultivate a generation equipped to face the challenges of the world with resilience, compassion, and integrity.

Families play a critical role in shaping the moral and ethical framework of individuals. From a young age, children learn fundamental life skills, social norms, and coping mechanisms through their family interactions. These early lessons influence their development and impact their behavior as adults, ultimately shaping the fabric of society. A society built on strong, nurturing families will have citizens who understand the importance of cooperation, empathy, and accountability.

Moreover, the family serves as the first institution that teaches the value of community and social responsibility. When parents model good behavior and instill a sense of duty and respect for others, children are more likely to carry those lessons into their adult lives. This creates a cycle of positive behavior that spreads throughout communities, helping to address social issues such as crime, inequality, and poverty.

Building a new society through family is crucial for the long-term stability and prosperity of any nation. This is because the family unit is the primary environment where individuals develop emotionally, socially, and psychologically. A supportive and nurturing family foundation fosters positive self-esteem, emotional intelligence, and resilience, essential qualities for personal well-being and societal contributions. Strong families also play a significant role in preventing social issues, such as substance abuse, criminal behavior, and teenage pregnancies, by providing children with guidance, boundaries, and support. Moreover, families contribute to economic stability by teaching financial responsibility and providing resources for educational growth, ensuring individuals can thrive and contribute meaningfully to society.

Additionally, families pass down cultural knowledge, values, and wisdom, preserving important traditions and fostering a sense of identity and belonging. This intergenerational exchange helps create a cohesive society, where individuals feel connected and grounded in their community. Families also encourage social responsibility, teaching individuals to care for others, contribute to the community, and be accountable for their actions, which leads to a more compassionate society. They provide a safety net for vulnerable members, such as the elderly and sick, reducing the burden on healthcare systems and social services.

Furthermore, families are often the first to support education and personal growth, helping children succeed academically and develop the skills needed for future success. A society with strong families will naturally have a more educated and innovative population, capable of addressing complex challenges. Families also contribute to the strengthening of communities by building trust, cooperation, and mutual support. When families thrive, communities become safer, more connected, and more supportive of one another.

To build a new society, we must therefore prioritize the well-being of families. This means supporting parents through education, resources, and policies that enable them to provide safe, nurturing environments for their children. By investing in families, we lay the groundwork for a society that values cooperation, stability, and progress. In doing so, we create a future where individuals can thrive, communities can prosper, and the nation can achieve its fullest potential.

In conclusion, a strong family foundation is key to building a new society, one that is emotionally healthy, socially responsible, economically stable, and culturally rich. By prioritizing the well-being of families, we are investing in the future of society itself.

GBENGA ANOLA

CHAPTER 2: MENTORING, COACHING, SHADOWING

Mentoring and coaching are widely utilized in corporate organizations and the business world to share knowledge and to foster growth and development. However, I believe that the concept of mentoring is critically needed for nation-building and the creation of a crime-free society. To build a better society, mentoring should extend to families, communities, and the society at large. Individuals must embrace mentoring, especially focusing on children from broken homes (children from divorced or separated homes), to provide emotional guidance and ensure they are not neglected. The increasing prevalence of broken homes has become a significant issue in society, and the primary victims of divorce and separation are the innocent children who often endure psychological trauma and profound emotional pain. While not all children from such families negatively impact society, research indicates that many experience emotional trauma and feelings of neglect, which can lead to depression and other behavioral issues. Mentorship, a process that can be initiated by either the mentors or the mentees, offers a solution to this crisis by providing stability and guidance, thereby addressing the root causes of insecurity.

To tackle the growing insecurity in our nation, mentoring is essential within families. The high divorce rate in the United States—approximately 50%—and the prevalence of single-parent households (80% of which are headed by mothers) highlight the urgent need for support. While single mothers often do their best, certain challenges may require a father figure or additional mentorship. Teenagers from single-parent homes often lose out on values that contribute to positive behavior, increasing their vulnerability to negative influences such as drug cartels, gangs, and criminal activities.

Creating a safe society therefore requires adopting mentoring as a societal norm, particularly for teenagers from single-parent families. Such children are at a higher risk of engaging in defiant behaviors. Mentoring can help fill the gaps left by single parenting, providing essential guidance, emotional stability, and a framework for developing positive values. A proactive approach to mentoring can prevent these children from becoming societal threats and instead nurture them into responsible and productive individuals.

Father Abandons His Family

Consider a scenario where a father abandons his family, taking vital documents and draining the family's savings. I would be so happy if I could tell you that this is just my imagination running wild, but no, these are real life experiences of people! Such a family is left in financial and emotional disarray, with children facing immense psychological pressure and an uncertain future. Growing up in such circumstances increases the likelihood of these children developing behavioral issues. Mentoring can play a transformative role in such situations by offering emotional support, academic assistance, skill development, and exposure to positive networks. A mentor can act as a father figure, helping children set goals, build self-esteem, and navigate life's challenges.

To ensure a secure and thriving future, society must embrace mentoring as a collective responsibility. By addressing the needs of children from broken homes and providing them with the guidance and support they lack, mentoring can help build a world that is safe, inclusive, and free from insecurity.

What Actually Is Mentoring?

A researcher defines mentoring as a form of social support provided by a skilled individual to someone less experienced. Mentoring represents a long-term relationship between a more experienced person and a less experienced one. While the term is often associated with the corporate or business world, its meaning, however, extends beyond professional settings. Mentoring can involve activities as diverse as helping a child learn to read, guiding a young person in engaging with constructive programs, or offering vocational and career advice. You would agree with me that these are greatly needed in society.

Mentoring can take many forms, from brief, occasional interactions between unrelated individuals to the formation of deep, long-term emotional connections. These relationships may exist between individuals of the same or different genders, races, or ethnic backgrounds. Mentoring has proven to benefit many children, and there is potential for even more young people to be supported through mentorship, a need that is increasingly vital in today's society.

This book seeks to explore all available strategies to reduce crime, with a particular focus on the role of families and mentoring. It emphasizes the importance of mentoring in fostering healthy behavior and preventing health and social issues, particularly among children from disadvantaged or broken families. It is worth noting that children from broken homes have a more numerous and intense level of emotion, experience more emotional disturbances, are more aggressive, less independent, and less responsive to others. This has tendencies to affect the performance of the children in school due to the fact that their emotions are tied up with divorce and emotional trauma. Some of these children thus become truant, delinquent, and often place little or no emphasis on continuing their education. The ineffectiveness of family reinforcement makes the mentoring and buddy system crucial for these underprivileged children.

The children in these homes struggle with their self-esteem, and they are more emotionally unstable, more likely to feel unhappy, and tend to experience more emotional stress. This is simply because the family that is meant to provide love, protection and a sense of belonging, which a child needs to develop into a mature and well-adjusted adult, has broken apart. This book is therefore greatly needed at this point, with the growing rate of divorce all over the world especially in Europe and America, which has directed the entire society to the tremendous impact of broken homes on the human race. I therefore encourage that every part of this book be properly read and digested so we can begin an era of nation building.

Government And Parent Partnership In Mentoring

When two parents agree to divorce or separate, the government is typically notified, and the separation is formally recognized. In most cases, the father is summoned to provide financial support in the form of child support payments. However, there is often no provision for addressing the child's emotional needs, nor is there any guidance offered for the many challenges they may face, such as educational struggles, health issues, or other life difficulties. This leaves an important question unanswered: Who provides the necessary guidance and emotional support to help these children navigate such a difficult situation? Tragically, many innocent children are left to endure this traumatic experience on their own.

This gap in the divorce and separation process highlights the urgent need for reform. While financial support is essential, it is only one aspect of a child's well-being.

Emotional support and guidance must also be prioritized to ensure that children from divorced or separated homes do not feel abandoned or neglected. These children require a holistic approach that addresses all facets of their lives, including mental health, education, social development, and resilience-building.

To achieve this, governments and policymakers must consider implementing systems that extend beyond financial obligations. For instance, mandatory counseling or therapy sessions for children of divorced parents could help them process their emotions and cope with the changes in their family structure. Schools and community organizations could provide mentorship programs, pairing these children with supportive adults who can offer guidance and serve as positive role models. Additionally, parents undergoing divorce should be encouraged or even required to participate in co-parenting workshops that focus on maintaining a united front for the benefit of their children.

Another critical area of reform is ensuring that children have access to resources tailored to their unique needs. Educational support programs could help children stay focused on their studies despite the upheaval in their personal lives. Healthcare services should include access to mental health professionals who specialize in dealing with the effects of divorce on children. Furthermore, social services could step in to provide a safety net for families struggling to meet their children's basic needs, ensuring that no child is left behind due to the financial or emotional strain of a divorce.

Ultimately, the process of divorce or separation should prioritize the long-term well-being of the children involved. This means creating a framework that addresses not only financial support but also emotional guidance, educational assistance, and healthcare. By doing so, society can ensure that these children are equipped to overcome the challenges they face and emerge as resilient, well-rounded individuals. Reforming the divorce and separation process in this way is not just a legal necessity—it is a moral imperative to protect society's most vulnerable members.

Psychological Effects Of Broken Homes Or Separation On Children

Children from broken homes are often left feeling abandoned. They experience emotional challenges due to the effects of separation, leading to psychological issues that stem from a sense of abandonment, even if both parents are alive (and physically present). True abandonment arises from the distance created by emotional indifference—a deeper form of neglect that occurs not from physical absence but from emotional disconnection. In this context, **emotional indifference** refers to a lack of care, concern, or involvement. When a person becomes emotionally indifferent, they stop engaging, even if they are physically present.

This type of abandonment is often more painful because it involves feeling neglected, ignored, or emotionally unsupported by someone who may still be physically present but has emotionally distanced themselves. It highlights the idea that true abandonment isn't always about physical absence; it can stem from a withdrawal of affection, attention, and emotional intimacy.

Some Coaching And Mentorship Models

Coaching, in the form of education, is essential for both parents and children from divorced or separated homes. It is important to note that divorce presents unique challenges for both parents and children, necessitating targeted support to address these difficulties. Educational and support programs for parents are effective interventions that help them co-parent, understand age-appropriate ways to support their children, and develop healthier coping mechanisms. By teaching parents how to manage conflict and communicate effectively with their children, these programs reduce parental disputes and minimize the negative emotional impact on children. When parents remain calm and stable, they provide a critical layer of support, helping their children navigate the divorce process with less exposure to conflict and stress.

Community-supported programs also play a pivotal role in breaking cycles of conflict and poor coping mechanisms within families. They help parents enhance communication with their children, foster resilience, and meet their children's emotional needs. As a result, children are better equipped to cope with adversity, reducing their likelihood of engaging in criminal behavior in the long term. A Midwest case study demonstrated reduced criminality among children whose families participated in county-based education and support programs. While some participants were mandated to attend, the significant number of repeat participants underscores the community's recognition of the value these services offer. With the increasing divorce rates across the United States, the demand for such programs continues to grow, highlighting their importance in promoting healthier family dynamics and supporting children during and after divorce.

Identifiable mentorship programs play a crucial role

in supporting children, particularly those from broken homes, by addressing both their academic and emotional needs. **Traditional school-based mentoring programs** can provide not only academic support but also preventive measures against drug and alcohol abuse, violence, and conflict. Such programs focus on fostering healthy communication skills and coping mechanisms, helping children avoid negative paths and lead healthier lives. Similarly, **tutoring programs** offer assistance in core subjects like reading, writing, and mathematics, helping children cope with academic stress while providing emotional reassurance. These programs offer a stable source of guidance, enabling children to focus on their personal and academic growth.

Campus-based programs further bridge the gap between schools, colleges, communities, and industries by offering a combination of academic tutoring, extracurricular activities, and college preparation. They foster positive relationships between children and adults, enhancing self-esteem, social skills, and career preparedness, particularly for children from broken homes. Additionally, **father-mother figure programs** address the absence of strong parental figures by creating one-on-one mentorships that simulate a parent-child relationship. These mentors provide emotional stability and guidance, helping children feel supported and cared for. Matching mentors with children based on personality traits ensures meaningful connections, offering the emotional foundation these children need to face life's challenges.

Each of these programs offers a structured approach to building resilience and brighter futures for children from broken homes. By implementing such initiatives in communities and organizations, we can collectively work toward a society free from crime, fostering hope and opportunity for all.

Shadowing

Shadowing plays a crucial role in shaping society because the image of society is often a reflection of the family. In other words, we can create the kind of society we envision, but that begins with what we model for our families—particularly for children, who will shape the future. Shadowing can be likened to a farmer sowing maize and expecting to harvest rice—an impossibility. It is evident that whatever seeds we plant in society today will determine what we reap tomorrow. The current state of society is a direct result of what has been sown, but we have the power to change this trajectory. Transforming society requires first changing the values and behaviors we instill within our families. The family is the focal point of society, and the attitudes parents display before their children will inevitably be replicated—often in greater measure.

This concept is well supported by psychological theories, particularly Albert Bandura's social learning theory (1977), which posits that individuals learn behaviors through observation, imitation, and modeling. In families where criminal behavior is present, children often engage in shadowing—closely observing and imitating the actions of family members involved in crime. This process can normalize deviant behavior and significantly increase the likelihood of criminal involvement. For example, a child who grows up watching a parent engage in theft, fraud, or drug dealing may come to see such behavior as acceptable or even as the only means of survival. Research further shows that children of incarcerated parents have a higher likelihood of engaging in criminal behavior compared to their peers from non-criminal families (Farrington et al., 2001). Similarly, a parent who exhibits aggression may inadvertently raise children who develop aggressive tendencies.

I have often heard my fellow correctional officers remark that after dealing with inmates all day, they find themselves becoming aggressive at home. My own daughter once told me about a part-time teacher at her school who had previously worked in a prison. One day, while teaching, some students were talking instead of paying attention. Frustrated, the teacher suddenly screamed at them, startling the entire class. Some students even fell to the floor in shock. Realizing what had happened, the teacher quickly apologized, explaining that he was used to working in a prison environment, where shouting was often necessary. This example highlights how behavioral patterns learned in one environment can unconsciously carry over into others —including into the home. If correctional officers and other professionals in high-stress environments are not mindful of their behaviors, their children may develop aggressive tendencies simply by observing and imitating them.

Shadowing is particularly significant because certain behaviors, once learned, can be passed down from generation to generation. This is why we often see a father serving time in prison, only for his children to end up incarcerated as well. Intergenerational transmission of crime can occur when children subconsciously follow in their parents' footsteps due to genetic, environmental, and social factors. Some studies suggest that antisocial behavior and aggression may have hereditary components. Additionally, growing up in a criminogenic environment—marked by poverty, violence, and instability—can reinforce criminal tendencies. Children exposed to trauma, neglect, and parental incarceration may struggle with emotional regulation, making them more vulnerable to delinquent behavior.

Children who shadow criminal parents may not only adopt their tactics and justifications for illegal activities but also internalize deviant behavior as a survival mechanism. This shadowing can manifest explicitly, such as through direct involvement in gang activity, or implicitly, through the normalization of fraud, violence, or other criminal behaviors as survival mechanisms. Research indicates that delinquency rates are significantly higher among youth with criminal parents or siblings. This underscores the urgent need for parents to model positive behaviors and values, as their attitudes and actions have a profound impact on their children's future.

Shadowing has far-reaching consequences for society. When negative behaviors are passed down, crime rates increase, recidivism is reinforced, and communities suffer the consequences. In many cases, misguided mentorship in society only exacerbates the problem. These realities call for a paradigm shift—a collective effort to break cycles of criminality by instilling positive values within families. If we want to see a transformed society, we must begin by transforming the family unit.

GBENGA ANOLA

CHAPTER 3: THE IMPACT OF GOVERNMENT AND ECONOMIC POLICIES ON CRIME

Government and economic policies play a significant role in influencing crime rates, particularly among youth. During economic downturns or when restrictive policies limit opportunities for individuals to thrive, crime rates tend to rise. This is especially true for crimes such as burglary and car theft, which are often linked to financial hardship and lack of access to resources. The relationship between the economy and crime is complex, but it is clear that economic instability contributes to higher youth involvement in criminal activities. When young people face financial uncertainty and hopelessness, they are more likely to resort to crime as a means of survival.

Both in Africa and Europe, the state of the economy heavily influences crime rates, largely due to widespread poverty and mismanagement of resources. A small group of individuals often controls the majority of national resources, leading to significant economic inequality. The inability of governments to address issues like unemployment exacerbates this problem, creating an environment where young people see little opportunity for a better future. As a result, many turn to illegal means to meet their needs. While children from single-parent households may statistically be more prone to crime, especially under these conditions, it is not always the case. Many single-parent families successfully raise well-behaved children, particularly when their needs are met and they are shielded from negative influences.

Economic pressures also affect parents, who may struggle to fulfill promises made to their children, leading to a sense of disappointment. This can drive children toward crime as they seek alternatives to meet their expectations. Governments have a responsibility to create a strong economy that enables all citizens, including the youth, to thrive. This involves ensuring that wealth and resources are not concentrated in the hands of a few. Additionally, parents must be mindful of the promises they make and the resources available to them, as unrealistic expectations can lead children to engage in criminal activity.

Several economic factors contribute to youth crime, including unemployment and a lack of educational opportunities. When young people are unable to find jobs or access quality education, they may feel frustrated and turn to crime. Governments must create an environment where industries thrive, generating employment opportunities for youth. Without jobs, many young people will inevitably resort to criminal alternatives for survival. Additionally, education plays a vital role in shaping a child's behavior and future prospects. If children lack access to quality education, they are less likely to acquire the skills needed for legitimate employment, making them more vulnerable to criminal behavior.

Both formal and informal education are crucial in shaping youth behavior. Social learning—what children learn from their environment—can strongly influence their development. If not properly guided, this informal learning can lead to criminal tendencies. Governments should support empowerment centers that provide practical training in various fields, such as IT, manufacturing, and healthcare, equipping young people with skills that improve their employability and reduce the likelihood of criminal behavior.

In conclusion, addressing economic challenges such as unemployment, lack of education, and unequal resource distribution is essential to preventing youth from engaging in crime. A strong, inclusive economy, coupled with appropriate educational opportunities and family support, is key to creating a safer society. Government policies must be designed to address the root causes of criminal behavior, rather than merely reacting to it after the fact. By focusing on the socio-economic factors that contribute to crime, governments can create a healthier, more secure society for all citizens.

The Issue Of Poverty And Inequality In Our Society

The relationship between socio-economic disadvantages and juvenile crime has been extensively studied in the United States, revealing a troubling connection. Research consistently shows that children living in poverty face a higher risk of exposure to various forms of violence. Juvenile offending is more prevalent among children from low-income families, whereas those from higher-income families experience the lowest rates of violent victimization. At the same time, children from financially disadvantaged backgrounds are more likely to become victims of crime. This correlation highlights the persistent link between poverty and higher rates of violence against children and adolescents. In particular, children from impoverished communities are more vulnerable to community violence, which increases their risk of engaging in criminal behavior.

Poverty also leads to profound psychological effects, such as feelings of desperation and helplessness, which make children more susceptible to antisocial behavior and academic failure. The documented connection between economic inequality and juvenile crime underscores how social comparisons can amplify perceptions of injustice, fostering a sense of disconnection and resentment. When individuals observe disparities in status, wealth, or opportunities, they may experience dissatisfaction and frustration. For some, this frustration manifests as criminal behavior, an attempt to "level the playing field" or express discontent with systemic inequities.

This sense of resentment is particularly acute in small, economically disadvantaged communities where resources are scarce. Among young people, who value fairness and equality, the perceived lack of justice in their environment often leads to deep-seated frustration. Over time, this frustration becomes difficult to overcome, especially in the absence of opportunities to improve their circumstances. Limited access to essential resources exacerbates this problem, increasing the likelihood of delinquent behavior.

To address these issues, a comprehensive strategy is required to reduce juvenile crime, especially during economic downturns when vulnerable families are most at risk. This strategy should include counter-cyclical development programs aimed at mitigating the effects of economic challenges. These programs must prioritize socio-economic interventions alongside traditional legal and punitive measures. By increasing public resource transfers to poorer families, children can be provided with access to constructive activities such as sports, music, and the arts.

Engaging in structured and enriching activities offers young people positive outlets for their energy and creativity, significantly reducing their likelihood of engaging in criminal behavior. This preventative approach targets the root causes of juvenile crime by focusing on financial support and creating opportunities for personal growth. By addressing poverty and inequality at their source, society can foster a safer, more equitable environment where all children can thrive.

Government Economic Policies And Their Impact

On Crime

Economic policies significantly influence the prevalence of crime among children, especially in urban areas. Rising poverty levels often correlate with increased juvenile delinquency. Studies reveal that communities with pronounced income inequality and high population turnover are more prone to elevated juvenile crime rates. In slum areas, where continuous excitement, group hostility, and mutual distrust prevail, a violent lifestyle often becomes normalized and passed from one individual to another—and from one generation to the next. This cycle ingrains crime as a way of life for many young people in these environments.

One primary reason underprivileged children are more likely than their wealthier counterparts to engage in illegal activities is their exclusion from the legal job market. Discrimination and a lack of accessible employment opportunities often force many to seek unlawful means to meet basic needs such as food, housing, and clothing. Stable, legal employment is essential for fulfilling these needs, but when legal pathways are blocked, desperation pushes many toward illegal alternatives.

Government and economic policies often exacerbate this problem by inadvertently creating conditions that push children toward crime. These policies must be critically examined for their principles, relevance, and impact on children and their families. The relationship between child-focused welfare initiatives and broader economic strategies plays a crucial role in shaping a family's financial stability and, ultimately, a child's likelihood of engaging in criminal behavior.

Historical examples highlight the unintended consequences of economic policies on juvenile crime. From 19th-century England to modern-day U.S. policies and global economic initiatives of the 1990s, governments have experienced both successes and failures in addressing the factors that drive children into delinquency. To tackle this issue effectively, a comprehensive approach is required—one that integrates economic stability, robust social support systems, and accessible opportunities for youth and their families. Such an approach would help break the cycle of poverty and crime, creating pathways for vulnerable children to thrive.

The Relevance Of Welfare Policies

Welfare policies are designed to address disparities in the market that place low-income families and their children at a disadvantage. These programs aim to provide financial assistance, food, housing, and medical care to those most in need. A key question arises: can welfare packages help reduce juvenile crime in the United States? From my experience as a correctional officer, it is clear that poverty is a major contributor to juvenile crime. I recall a conversation with an inmate who explained that he turned to drug trafficking because his mother could no longer support him and his sister. In an attempt to help his family, he was offered an opportunity to sell drugs, which led him down a criminal path.

Welfare programs, including income guarantee initiatives, aim to support families in raising children by providing financial stability. One such program, the Earned Income Tax Credit (EITC), has been shown to improve the lives of low-wage workers, offering a positive alternative to crime. The EITC, combined with the federal minimum wage, significantly increases the after-tax incentive for work. It also provides larger welfare checks to individuals with low wages, in cases where the EITC equals or exceeds their tax liability. Essentially, the EITC serves as a wage supplement for those who might otherwise be tempted to engage in illegal activities, such as drug trafficking, due to financial strain or a lack of opportunity.

Research has demonstrated that increased earnings from

the EITC can lead to better outcomes for children, including reduced infant mortality, lower rates of low birth weights, and improved overall health. Furthermore, EITC payments made directly to mothers following childbirth have been linked to improved child outcomes, such as better test scores. By providing financial stability and encouraging employment, welfare programs like the EITC can help reduce the pressures that often lead to criminal behavior, particularly among youth.

Accessibility To Education And Employment As A Means Of Curbing Crime

Educational policies must focus on integrating curricula that deter children from engaging in crime, identify potential risks they may face, and provide timely interventions. Access to education and job opportunities plays a vital role in crime prevention by equipping young people with the tools to become responsible adults. Education imparts not only knowledge but also practical skills, leading to better job prospects and higher wages, which reduce the likelihood of turning to crime to meet basic needs. Formal schooling provides essential socialization experiences that protect against delinquent behavior, but governments must also prioritize informal education, such as technical training and skill development programs, to ensure youth acquire employable skills. Policies should aim for equitable access to both formal and informal education through initiatives like scholarships and community outreach programs that prepare children for successful transitions into the workforce.

It is crucial to expand the focus beyond traditional academic education to include vocational training and technical certifications, ensuring they are equally valued. Programs emphasizing practical skills and hands-on work, like those implemented in many Western countries, offer alternative pathways for youth who struggle in conventional academic settings. These initiatives equip young people with marketable skills, reducing their risk of delinquency by providing viable employment opportunities. Research consistently shows a strong correlation between higher levels of education and lower rates of criminal behavior, while youth unemployment continues to be a significant driver of crime. When young people lack access to education or meaningful work, they are more likely to engage in illegal activities to survive.

Governments must develop comprehensive policies that encourage youth to remain in school longer, promote participation in vocational training programs, and provide hands-on experiences that blend theoretical education with practical, paid, or unpaid work opportunities. These efforts instill a sense of responsibility, offer alternatives to criminal behavior, and ensure that even those who face academic challenges have pathways to success. By addressing unemployment and equipping youth with workforce-ready skills, governments can substantially reduce crime rates and foster a safer, more secure society.

Essential Steps The Government Should Take

Addressing the systemic issues that contribute to juvenile crime, particularly those arising from inadequate government and economic policies, requires urgent and comprehensive reform. Effective solutions must adopt a broad and inclusive approach, tackling both localized community challenges and broader structural issues such as inequality, poverty, and unemployment. Local conditions focus on the specific needs of individual communities, while systemic conditions address the overarching socio-economic factors that influence entire regions or countries. A holistic view ensures that the root causes of juvenile crime are effectively addressed at all levels.

Policy reform should prioritize evidence-based approaches, evaluating and comparing various alternatives to identify the most effective strategies. By relying on proven methods, policies can be tailored to meet the diverse needs of children and families. Advocacy for reform should focus on solutions that have demonstrated success, ensuring interventions are both practical and sustainable.

This book underscores the critical importance of implementing evidence-based strategies in areas such as school readiness, access to quality healthcare, education, welfare support, and lifestyle improvement. These policies must be dynamic, adapting to new evidence and continually refined to maximize effectiveness. Improving access to education and enhancing job prospects through better wages are essential steps in preventing juvenile crime. Economic instability, welfare deficiencies, and family-related crises often push children out of the education system, increasing their vulnerability to criminal activities.

Children facing family disruptions or lacking educational opportunities frequently end up in youth detention centers or community correctional facilities, where their challenges often worsen. Time spent in custody can limit their skill development and reduce future employment prospects. To counter this, reform efforts must focus on re-engaging these children with the education system and equipping them with qualifications that lead to meaningful employment. A practical, skill-oriented approach to education, supported by investments in healthcare, welfare, and economic stability, can dramatically improve outcomes for at-risk youth.

Research highlights the strong connections between early education, preschool programs, and positive life outcomes. Comprehensive intervention policies not only transform the lives of vulnerable children but also provide long-term social and economic benefits. When viewed as a moral obligation, these policies become powerful instruments for building a safer, more equitable society.

CHAPTER 4: THE SECURITY CONCEPT THAT WINS

The world can be unpredictable and, at times, dangerous, filled with risks that may catch us off guard. Unfortunately, many Americans underestimate these dangers. However, it's important to take proactive steps as a family to prepare for potential risks—not just criminal threats, but also other hazards like car accidents, house fires, and weather-related emergencies. A good place to start is by having an open discussion about the challenges your family might face, and then working together to develop strategies to reduce or eliminate these risks. When crafting a plan to protect your family, think beyond the basics. Be imaginative and consider the wide range of threats you might encounter.

Once you've identified these risks, work together as a family to determine the best strategies to avoid, defend against, or respond to each one.

Taking a comprehensive approach is key. Address various aspects of security, including physical and digital protection, risk avoidance, site safety and fortification, regular security drills, and essential first-aid training. While physical security often demands the most attention, all these areas are crucial to creating a robust safety plan.

There are three core areas to focus on in creating a strong foundation for safety: physical security, digital security, and first-aid skills. In this guide, we'll explore practical steps to enhance the security of your family. Regardless of whether you live in a bustling city, a quiet suburb, or a rural area, crime and other risks can affect anyone—so it's essential to be prepared.

Why Security Should Be Part Of Family Discussions And Budgeting

Protecting our families is undeniably one of the most important priorities in life. Regardless of where you live, numerous threats can jeopardize your family's well-being and disrupt your lifestyle. These threats include crime, physical accidents, natural disasters, financial loss, health risks, and cyberbullying. Such dangers can create unsafe, unpredictable, and stressful environments for both children and adults. Families that neglect security measures often experience greater feelings of paranoia, worry, and insecurity compared to those who actively address these risks.

A threat management approach not only ensures physical safety but also promotes emotional and mental well-being. Its purpose extends beyond preparing families to respond to specific dangers; it emphasizes recognizing early warning signs and understanding the potential risks they may face. This proactive mindset fosters an alert and informed family environment.

Equally important is maintaining awareness of how each family member feels, as their emotional state can provide valuable insights into the family's overall vulnerability. By being attentive and understanding their concerns, you can identify areas that require attention to sustain a safe, positive, and supportive atmosphere for everyone.

Physical Security Measures For Your Family

Investing in effective security systems can significantly protect your family from potential threats, but starting with basic security measures is essential. Experts recommend that every home undergo a security assessment to identify vulnerabilities and areas needing improvement. With rising crime rates due to the current economic climate, prioritizing physical security has never been more important.

The first point of entry for most break-ins is the front gate, followed by visible areas like doors and windows. Burglars often assess homes for alarm systems and basic security devices that are easily noticeable. Addressing these elements creates a strong physical deterrent and promotes a safer environment. Let's get right into it!

How To Secure Your Home

Creating a secure home environment requires a combination of practical measures and regular maintenance. Below is a structured approach to enhance your home security:

1. Entry Point Security

Locks: Install high-quality deadbolt locks and bump-proof window locks. Regularly inspect and use them to ensure they remain effective.

Alarms: Opt for monitored alarm systems for round-the-clock protection. If a monitored system isn't feasible, consider loud alarms with strobe lights to deter intruders.

2. Deterrents and Visibility

Lighting: Ensure adequate lighting both inside and outside your home to deter criminals. Well-lit properties are less likely to be targeted.

Surveillance Systems: Place visible surveillance cameras, real or faux, to discourage potential burglars.

3. Property Maintenance

Landscaping: Trim trees, shrubs, and bushes near the house to eliminate hiding spots for intruders.

Fences, Gates, and Play Structures: Keep fences and gates in good repair. If you don't have these structures, consider installing them to improve security and define boundaries.

4. Ongoing Security Measures

Periodic Assessments: Conduct regular security audits to identify and address vulnerabilities, such as outdated locks or damaged hardware.

Smart Home Technology: Upgrade to smart devices, like smart locks and cameras, for enhanced monitoring and control.

5. Community Involvement

Neighborhood Watch: Active community engagement can significantly reduce crime rates. Establishing or joining a neighborhood watch program fosters a safer environment for everyone.

By implementing these measures and staying proactive, you can significantly improve the safety and security of your home.

The Reality Of Burglary Theft

Burglary theft is often an "inside job," committed by people who have access to information about you, such as neighbors or untrusted acquaintances. Burglars, like car thieves, are usually motivated by the prospect of quick financial gain. They may sell stolen goods to fund drug habits or other illegal activities. Burglars tend to be strategic, striking during the day when homeowners are likely to be at work or shopping, targeting empty homes to avoid direct confrontation.

I experienced burglary firsthand when my family's home was broken into while we were at church. After a large party the previous day, burglars saw an opportunity when the house was left unattended. They broke in through the back door and stole clothes, shoes, watches, and other valuables. The first sign of trouble was the back door being open—though we had locked it before leaving for church.

Burglars often use deceptive tactics to scout homes, such as posing as salespeople or delivery persons to gauge whether anyone is home. They might leave flyers on your door and return later to see if they've been removed, or they may knock on your door, pretending to look for someone. If no one answers, they take the opportunity to break in.

The absence of neighbors can also encourage burglaries, as quiet streets provide burglars with the cover they need. Community integration can be an effective deterrent against such crimes. If neighbors look out for each other, it becomes harder for criminals to strike unnoticed. Additionally, having a dog, no matter how small, can deter burglars. Installing security systems like alarms and cameras can also help deter burglars and assist in tracking and apprehending them if a break-in occurs.

In summary, criminals are always on the lookout for opportunities to exploit. Whether it's snatching a bag, stealing a car, or breaking into a home, they rely on moments of vulnerability. Staying alert, taking precautions, and fostering a strong community can significantly reduce the risk of becoming a victim.

Adhering To Personal Security Tips

Aligning ourselves to basic security is vital to our existence as a family. Safety concerns extend beyond the home, making it essential for family members to stay vigilant and well-prepared in public spaces. Activities such as commuting to work or school, shopping, or traveling can present potential risks. Being aware of escape routes in both public and private areas, as well as understanding how to respond during natural disasters or societal emergencies, is crucial.

In workplaces and other public settings, situational awareness and basic self-defense skills are vital. Regularly altering daily routines and avoiding predictability can reduce the likelihood of being targeted by criminals. Staying alert and observant sends a clear message to potential perpetrators that you are not an easy target.

For those unable to physically defend themselves, such as women and children, learning self-defense techniques, including martial arts, can be particularly empowering.

Modern technology also offers useful tools, such as safety apps that alert monitoring parties when help is needed. These apps are especially important when others are unaware of your location, as communication lapses can delay assistance.

By integrating these practices into your daily life, you can develop a proactive safety mindset to protect yourself and your family. Relying solely on home security measures without taking precautions in the outside world can leave you vulnerable. A balanced approach to safety ensures comprehensive protection.

Inside And Outside Security Lifestyle

Concerns about security have become a global issue, affecting people across the world: everyone often experiences anxiety about their personal safety in various locations—whether at school, grocery stores, restaurants, churches, mosques, event centers, or any other public place.

Security challenges are now a global phenomenon, impacting the West, Asia, America, and Canada alike. Many of the most advanced technologies today are developed primarily to combat and track crime in society, including metal detectors, tracking devices, and electronic surveillance systems. These tools, used by law enforcement agencies, aim to monitor and prevent criminal activities. Yet, despite these advancements, the world still feels increasingly unsafe, making it difficult for families to feel secure. Nowadays, even something as simple as planning a vacation often involves researching the safety of the destination, reflecting the troubling state of our world. A tragic example of this took place at a *Kurdish Cultural Center* in Paris, where a 69-year-old French man carried out a mass shooting aimed at foreigners. The attack claimed three lives and sparked protests, as it occurred just before the 10th anniversary of the killings of three Kurdish women activists in the same neighborhood. The suspect was eventually arrested, but the event highlighted the persistent danger and insecurity people face, even in highly developed nations.

Despite the introduction of new laws and cutting-edge equipment to combat crime, insecurity continues to thrive. This reality concerns all segments of society, rich and poor, educated and uneducated, white and black. This ongoing struggle should prompt us to place God at the center of our security efforts. Trusting in God does not lessen the importance of physical defense; rather, it reinforces it. The Bible says in Psalm 127:1, *"Unless the Lord builds the house, the builders labor in vain; unless the Lord watches over the city, the guards stand watch in vain."* We must adopt the faith of Shadrach, Meshach, and Abednego, who believed that their God was able to save them (Daniel 3:17–18). However, as already highlighted, trusting in God's protection is not a license for carelessness or complacency. At the tomb of Lazarus, Jesus told the people to roll away the stone before He raised Lazarus from the dead (John 11:39). He did this because He knew they had the ability to move the stone, while He performed the miracle they could not. Similarly, God's promises do not absolve us of our responsibilities; we must blend our faith with action. Faith without works is incomplete, and we are called to do our part while trusting God to do what we cannot.

Everyday, security is often overlooked as people go about their daily routines, rarely paying attention to potential dangers in their surroundings. Just because yesterday was safe doesn't mean today will be. One key fact to understand about security violations is that they are committed by human beings, just like us, who have emotions, thoughts, and motivations. However, many of these individuals are under influences—whether psychological, sociological, or environmental—that make them act irrationally and violate the safety of others.

In my experience interacting with inmates, I've realized that many of the so-called criminals are far more fearful than one might imagine. For instance, I've seen prisoners become anxious and submissive despite their earlier displays of aggression. When given orders, they comply quickly, trying to avoid potential consequences. It is essential to remember that criminals are first and foremost human beings who have been shaped by their environment, often through exposure to drugs or feelings of being wronged by society. These influences play a significant role in their criminal behavior.

Measures Required For Digital Security

While ensuring your family's physical well-being is crucial, it's equally important to address vulnerabilities in the digital world. Most family members use smartphones, laptops, or tablets daily to check emails, browse the web, or shop online. While these activities may seem harmless, they can expose personal information to risks like phishing attacks, adware, and malicious downloads.

Fortunately, there are effective digital security measures you can adopt to protect your family from these threats. Cybersecurity involves various tools and strategies, but the most critical step is internal education. Teach your family members to recognize and avoid potential threats.

Phishing attacks, for example, often appear as emails asking for sensitive personal information. Encourage your family to ignore suspicious emails, avoid clicking on unknown links, and never interact with unverified senders. Additionally, caution everyone against downloading software from unauthorized or untrusted sources.

To enhance protection, schedule regular antimalware scans on all devices. While these measures are essential, the best defense lies in consistently practicing good security habits. Educating your household members about these practices ensures they can safeguard their own devices and data. By following these guidelines, you can reduce the risk of digital vulnerabilities and protect the personal information of everyone in your household.

Effective password management is one of the most crucial ways to protect your family in the digital age. Every account on every website is a potential target, as some sites offer stronger security measures than others. Creating strong, unique passwords is therefore a critical first step in safeguarding your personal information. A robust password can act as a powerful barrier against breaches, preventing unauthorized access to sensitive data.

To ensure optimal security, it's essential to assign a unique password to each account. This way, if one password is compromised, it won't jeopardize other accounts. Additionally, passwords should be stored securely and shared only with trusted partners or guardians when necessary. Never share passwords openly on social media or other public platforms.

Regular password updates are crucial. Changing passwords every quarter is a recommended practice, even if you haven't noticed any suspicious activity. Many people think, "No one has accessed my account, so I don't need to change my password." However, regular updates reduce the risk of long-term vulnerabilities, especially since hackers often wait months before exploiting stolen credentials.

Two-factor authentication (2FA) adds another layer of protection. By requiring a second identifier, such as a code sent to a smartphone, 2FA ensures that even if a password is compromised, access to your accounts remains restricted.

In the event of a known breach, immediate action is necessary. Change affected passwords right away to prevent further exploitation. By staying vigilant and proactive with password management, you can help secure your family's digital presence and minimize risks.

The Traits Of Criminals

Criminals are typically opportunistic, always on the lookout for situations they can exploit. They often act impulsively, without thoroughly considering the consequences or risks. For example, a criminal may spot a woman dressed in expensive clothes, carrying multiple bags, and assume she has valuable items like money or a phone. Driven by this assumption, the criminal may attempt to snatch her bag without planning an escape route or thinking about the consequences.

In one case, a man who attempted a robbery in an area already under police surveillance found himself in trouble. He did not realize that security operatives were stationed nearby due to an earlier clash between communities following the murder of an activist. As he tried to snatch the woman's bag, her screams attracted bystanders and alerted the police. The criminal, unaware of the security presence, was soon apprehended, sustaining injuries in the process. This example highlights how many criminals fail to think through their actions or consider the potential risks.

Unlike street criminals who act on impulse, terrorists

take time to carefully plan their attacks. A terrorist might spend months, or even years, preparing for a single act of violence, making them distinct from petty criminals. Nevertheless, criminals are always on the lookout for opportunities to strike, especially targeting those who appear vulnerable. For example, women carrying bags and walking alone in public can become easy targets. To avoid being a victim, it's important to stay aware of your surroundings and be cautious if someone seems to be following you. If you're unsure about your safety, consider stopping in a well-lit, populated area to assess the situation.

Similarly, as a correctional officer, it's crucial not to allow inmates to walk directly behind you, as they may have harmful intentions. In any environment, staying aware of those around you can help prevent becoming a victim.

The 3 C's Of Personal Security

To avoid becoming a victim of crime, there are three essential traits to develop: **Confidence**, **Courage**, and **Coordination**.

I recall a time when I was at home with my family, working on an exam on my laptop, when suddenly, a loud banging came from the garage door. My children, frightened by the noise, ran to my room for safety. My wife and I, equally startled, initially felt helpless, unsure of who—or what—was causing the disturbance. Despite the shock, I regained my composure and first submitted my exam before investigating the source of the noise. Upon checking, I found that neighborhood kids were playing a game and had banged on the door by mistake. This situation highlights how our reactions to potential security threats are observed by our children, and the importance of staying calm, confident, and coordinated during such events.

To avoid becoming a victim in different environments— whether at home, school, or public places like restaurants —you must adopt the following attitudes, the 3 C's of personal security:

- **Confidence**: Attackers often target those who appear weak or afraid. A confident person, on the other hand, can deter potential threats. Learning self-defense skills like karate, taekwondo, or judo can help build confidence. Women, in particular, can benefit from projecting confidence through their body language. Walk with your head held high, shoulders back, and make eye contact to scan your surroundings. This sends a signal to would-be attackers that you are not an easy target.

- **Courage**: In moments of insecurity, having the courage to act can be a game changer. For example, after hearing the banging on my garage door, I calmly assessed the situation by checking the security lights and ensuring no one was trying to break in. Upon realizing it was children playing, I felt reassured. Courage allows you to take the necessary steps to ensure your safety without being paralyzed by fear.

- **Coordination**: Effective coordination involves using your body efficiently to respond to a threat. This means quickly assessing the situation, moving with purpose, and selecting the right actions at the right time. In a chaotic or dangerous situation, being well-coordinated can help you escape or protect yourself and others more effectively.

Preventing Auto Theft

Car theft remains a prevalent crime, with thieves targeting vehicles for monetary gain, joyrides, or other illicit activities. In some cases, they may use weapons to intimidate victims, capitalizing on the fact that people are more likely to prioritize their personal safety over their property. However, most car thieves act opportunistically, seeking situations with minimal risk.

For example, criminals often take advantage of scenarios where drivers leave their vehicles running unattended —such as while paying for gas or picking up takeout—especially in isolated areas at night. Despite advancements in anti-theft technology, such as GPS tracking systems, vehicles are still stolen regularly. Fortunately, these technologies have contributed to a decline in theft rates and improved recovery efforts for stolen cars.

To safeguard your vehicle from theft, consider these practices:

- **Never leave your car running unattended:** Even a brief absence creates an easy opportunity for theft.

- **Always turn off the engine and lock the doors:** Modern vehicles are more secure against theft without keys, as traditional hotwiring methods have become largely obsolete.

- **Park in well-lit, populated areas:** Thieves are less likely to target vehicles in visible and busy locations.

- **Stay aware of your surroundings:** Be cautious of unfamiliar individuals lingering near your car, particularly in isolated or dimly lit areas.

- **Invest in additional security measures:** Tools like

steering wheel locks, immobilizers, and alarm systems can serve as effective deterrents.

Law enforcement agencies manage a broad range of responsibilities, from combating drug trafficking to addressing public safety threats. While they work to prevent auto theft, personal responsibility is key. By implementing these simple yet effective precautions, you can significantly reduce the risk of becoming a victim and protect your vehicle from theft.

Choosing A Safe Seat In Public Places

One of my instructors, a pianist, once shared his habit of thinking through how long it would take him to react to an active shooter if one entered the church while he was playing the piano. His story highlights the importance of situational awareness in public places.

People often overlook potential threats while out and about, assuming their surroundings are safe. However, even in everyday settings like restaurants or public events, it's crucial to remain aware of your surroundings. While we trust in divine protection, as the Israelites did in Egypt (Exodus 12:1-13), we also have a responsibility to take practical steps to ensure our safety.

Before choosing a seat in a public space, consider

conducting a **Situational Awareness Analysis (SAA)**. This will help you select a secure seat and be better prepared in case of an emergency. Key points to consider include:

- **Scanning the room:** Observe the people around you, their behavior, and any potential risks.

- **Avoiding proximity to entrances:** Sitting farther from the entrance provides more time to react in a dangerous situation.

- **Choosing a seat with a view of exits:** This allows you to monitor who enters and exits while planning your escape route if needed.

- **Sitting strategically:** opt for a seat against a wall, facing the room, to maintain visibility and to move quickly if necessary.

- **Staying near a secondary exit:** A secondary exit may offer a faster and safer escape during an emergency.

- **Minimizing distractions:** While enjoying your time, remain mindful of your surroundings to stay prepared.

By incorporating these practices, you can enhance your personal safety and that of those around you, ensuring a more secure experience in public spaces.

Finally, prioritize choosing a seat that allows for quick and easy movement in case you need to leave swiftly. While restaurant staff may assign you a table for convenience, don't hesitate to request a different seat if it feels safer. Staying situationally aware, even in familiar settings, is crucial for protecting your safety and that of your family.

GBENGA ANOLA

CHAPTER 5: HOW PARENTS AND SOCIETY CAN FIGHT RADICALIZATION

*R*adicalization of children is not a new phenomenon in society; it has existed for ages and has multiple dimensions, including historical, sociological, and political dimensions. However, the radicalization of children has evolved over centuries and is often tied to various forms of ideological indoctrination and exploitation. The question is: what does child radicalization mean for a parent?

Let's take a look at the historic side of radicalization amongst children. Throughout history, children have often been indoctrinated into the dominant ideologies of their societies. In ancient civilizations, for example, Spartan boys in Greece were trained from a young age to be warriors, embracing a strict militaristic ideology. Religious indoctrination is another form of radicalization that children have faced across societies. Historically, many religious movements have involved the indoctrination of children to advance their belief systems. Colonial powers and imperial forces often used education as a tool for ideological imposition— Missionary schools and residential schools, for instance, were systems used to impose ideological concepts on indigenous children. These systems go all out to radicalize children into the dominant culture's ideology, often at the expense of their native traditions.

The radicalization of children is not just an ancient phenomenon—it remains deeply embedded in modern history. In the 20th century, during World War II, both Nazi Germany and the Soviet Union targeted children for ideological indoctrination. A prime example is the Hitler Youth in Nazi Germany, where children were trained in fascist ideology and militarism. Similarly, during post-colonial movements, certain revolutionary and guerrilla groups recruited child soldiers, exposing them to radical ideologies to further political missions. These children were often used in combat and propaganda efforts, shaping their beliefs to align with militant causes. Some governments and organizations have also used education systems to indoctrinate children into political ideologies, as seen in Maoist China and Cold War-era regimes.

In the 21st century, extremist groups like ISIS, Boko Haram, and others in conflict zones actively radicalize children, using them as fighters or propagandists. They exploit vulnerable youth through coercion, propaganda, and indoctrination in schools and on online platforms. With the rise of the internet, children are increasingly susceptible to radicalization through online forums, social media, and extremist content. Parents must therefore take an active interest in the websites their children visit.

Terrorist propaganda and indoctrination can reach a large audience in a short time, significantly influencing vulnerable individuals. Children and young people are particularly susceptible to radical ideologies. Reports indicate that minors account for more than 40% of all known cases of recruitment into Islamic terrorism today. In Italy alone, a sizable number of vulnerable minors are targeted by radicalized recruiters. Research suggests that children and adolescents may be more prone to radicalization than adults.

Understanding why some young people develop extreme

beliefs and engage in extremist activities is crucial. Psychological, social, and micro- and macro-level factors help explain this phenomenon. Human beings have a natural tendency to conform to authority, often adopting the views, religion, and ideology of their immediate community. Children, in particular, seek simple solutions to complex issues and may struggle to differentiate between various religious and ideological perspectives. At around age 12, children begin to develop more critical and sometimes negative views toward society. They distance themselves from parental influence and seek belonging in youth groups, which can increase their exposure to radical ideologies. Communication challenges often arise during this stage. If parents, educators, or others in a child's environment notice behavioral changes or signs of radicalization, these should not be ignored. Instead, individuals within the child's social network must remain available for dialogue and support.

Researchers identify two distinct forms of radicalization: the politically motivated extremism and religiously motivated extremism. While these forms share some characteristics, they also have unique features. In Western Europe, radicalization is often linked to the growing Muslim population and ongoing debates about civil and multicultural society. Some extremists aim to overthrow oppressive regimes, while others seek to enforce their interpretation of religious principles. Additionally, lone-actor extremists remain under-researched, highlighting a gap in counter-radicalization efforts. Research indicates that approximately 50% of young individuals who carried out terrorist acts were killed. Many attempted to join terrorist organizations but were unable to do so for various reasons. Additionally, studies show that a significant number of lone actors lacked the technical knowledge to construct their explosive devices.

Factors That Greatly Contribute To Children's Radicalization

Research has revealed that several factors contribute to children's radicalization. These factors may include individual factors, such as specific personality traits or cognitive development, as well as high susceptibility to peer pressure. In my view, social factors play a major role in influencing children: factors such as authoritarian parenting styles or negative political socialization within the family or the surrounding community can increase a child's susceptibility to radicalization.

Other radicalization factors may include the child's desire for autonomy and identity development, especially in combination with social exclusion, living in a community with a negative perspective because of its socio-economic situation, or being of a mixed background of different nationalities and cultures, thereby being under conflicting influences. Additionally, conflict situations such as war between religious groups, the loss of father or friends, or other violent events, followed by experiences of insecurity, will increase children's vulnerability to radicalization. Many children who are indoctrinated to believe in the superiority of their own religion and have prejudices against others are more likely to engage in violent acts.

To be able to effectively prevent any kind of radicalization, it is important to understand how the process of radicalization begins and the conditions that contribute to its formation and persistence. Research on this area reveals that the dominant model of radicalization largely follows a linear process—from the adoption of extremist views, which happens through attachment to a violent ideology or group, people are led to show a higher degree of threat and willingness to engage in violent acts. However, results of field research and case studies suggest a more complex model in which multiple factors interact with each other to create the potential conditions necessary for radicalization.

Some Ways To Prevent Children's Radicalization

This book would have done a grossly incomplete work on this concept of radicalization if ways to prevent radicalism in children and young people are not discussed. Let's see a few ways to do this.

Parents must be aware of their child's interests, social networks—including digital platforms—and remain attentive to any behavioral changes. These changes may signal the early stages of radicalization, and early intervention can provide timely support.

It is also crucial to recognize the potential consequences of harmful influences and dangerous associations, particularly in cases where a child has already been exposed to radical ideologies. Parents should engage their children in open conversations while maintaining awareness of their friendships and societal interests. They must also demonstrate confidence in their child's ability to resist external pressures.

Equally important is fostering discussions about diversity, social structures, and skepticism in a constructive manner. A child who strongly rejects differing viewpoints, democratic values, or critical thinking may be difficult to challenge. However, helping them develop essential skills—such as critical thinking, ethical reasoning (values), and responsible decision-making—can strengthen their ability to resist harmful ideologies.

Parents' Role In Preventing Children's Radicalization

Parents play a crucial role in preventing radicalization in their children. It is the fundamental concern of all parents to keep their children safe from harm, but they need not stop at the basic physical protection. First, parents are key in the prevention of radicalization and this is core to their central role as parents. When radicals target kids, teenagers, and young adults to try to recruit them to their cause, parents serve as the first line of defense. They may also be consulted by government counter-radicalization departments, the media, and other organizations. Moreover, parents can help identify their children to others—teachers, professionals, monitors, e.t.c—who may play a role in preventing radicalization. The case of Dennis Rader in Kansas USA, also known as BTK Killer (BTK—Blind, Torture, Kill), comes to mind. Dennis Rader embarked on several murders from 1974 to 1991, escaping arrest for decades whilst taunting authorities with letters detailing his crimes. His arrest in 2005 marked the resolution of one of the most notorious serial killer cases in American history. The breakthrough in the case occurred when Rader resumed communication with law enforcement, sending them a floppy disk that contained metadata linking him to a computer at the church where he worked. A crucial development came when Rader's daughter, Kerri Rawson, consented to investigators using her DNA to confirm a familial match to evidence left at the crime scenes. Her cooperation was instrumental in solidifying the case against her father. This case is an example of an investigation involving close family ties, highlighting the role of family involvement in criminal investigations, and demonstrating the difficult emotional and moral dilemmas relatives face when a loved one is implicated in a crime. While Kerri Rawson was not responsible for exposing her father's identity, her decision to assist law enforcement played a significant role in confirming his guilt.

There are several specific protections that parents can provide for their children against radicalization. This includes understanding the activities of children— including observing and analyzing the factors that might shape a child's thinking such as social environment, peer groups, or online content—and identifying sources of negative or extremist influence that could push a child toward harmful beliefs or behaviors. Furthermore, parents are to teach children critical thinking and resilience so they can recognize and resist harmful or manipulative messaging, and equally encourage open dialogue so as to be able to discuss and debunk radical ideas before they take root in the children. Parents should create an environment with close social support, so that children do not seek a feeling of belonging in inappropriate places. Also, close and trusted adults who have contact with their children can also be on the lookout for signs of radicalization when necessary.

The family is the first barrier to radicalization and terrorism, however parents who are worried that their child might be getting involved in radical activities will be far too afraid if the only counter-radicalization agents are national or local police agencies. *It is therefore worthy of note that the involvement of schools, health and social services, religious leaders and youth clubs, as well as local education authorities, is important in sustaining counter-radicalization.*

Why A Strong Parent-Child Relationship Is Necessary

Monica Lloyd explains that building "protective factors" can help prevent radicalization, and one key factor is fostering strong, trusting relationships. Experts agree that feelings of inadequacy, fear, or weak connections with authority figures, such as parents or caregivers, often contribute to radical behavior.

Positive relationships with parents can enhance a child's emotional intelligence, helping them understand and manage their emotions while interacting positively with others. This emotional intelligence enables children to express distress about personal or social challenges, reducing the likelihood of adopting hostile attitudes or stereotypes.

Studies show that parents significantly influence young people, especially those drawn to far-right ideologies. Parents who share open and supportive communication, offer emotional support, and participate in decision-making can help their children navigate dilemmas and avoid violence. This approach involves flexibility, listening, and encouraging open discussions, allowing children to develop healthy, pro-social perspectives. Such strong, dynamic relationships provide a foundation for guiding children through challenges and promoting their growth into emotionally resilient individuals.

The Role Of Society In Preventing Radicalization

Society plays a key role in preventing radicalization

and violent extremism by fostering connections and inclusivity. Building relationships between people from different backgrounds can reduce feelings of exclusion, especially for children and families. Communities can help by encouraging children to join activities like sports or clubs and by identifying those at risk. Programs that raise awareness, educate people on prevention, and support individuals and families affected by radicalization have been implemented in many countries. Community programs create safe, supportive environments where children can thrive. Efforts to counter radical content online and train young people to think critically about extremist ideas are essential. Schools, colleges, and youth projects provide anti-radical awareness training to empower young people.

Collaboration between governments, schools, social services, and local organizations is necessary to address the issue. Local groups need resources and support to respond effectively to violent extremism. National and international efforts are also critical to increasing community resilience and promoting shared messages against radicalization. A united approach involving education, family, health, and social services helps build a comprehensive system to prevent extremism and promote inclusion.

Conclusively, it is suggested that in order to break the cycle of radicalization, we need to stop the development of risk and resilience factors in our children, as radicalization simply does not happen in a vacuum. This book has therefore supported a broader inclusion of all children in our efforts to prevent violent radicalization, not just those already at risk of radicalization. So far, we have emphasized in this chapter the importance of considering both family and society in addressing child radicalization. The chapter also highlights the need to understand the psychosocial factors that contribute to radicalization and suggests that preventing the development of risk and resilience factors in children is key to breaking the cycle of radicalization. The chapter advocates including all children in efforts to prevent radicalization, not just those already at risk. Research should explore children's experiences to identify protective factors that promote safety. A twofold intervention approach is proposed: first, protect all children by addressing general risk factors, and second, focus on those exhibiting problematic behaviors, addressing root causes rather than using punitive measures. Special attention to child rights is necessary, especially in relation to violent radicalization and terrorism. Monitoring interventions and developing a robust evidence base will help guide policies to prevent the emergence of violent extremists.

Radicalization In Prisons: Causes And Prevention

Introduction

Over the past two decades, the issue of radicalization within prison settings has become a significant concern for policymakers and academics alike. Prisons in many countries are increasingly regarded as breeding grounds for extremist ideologies, prompting both calls for stringent measures to combat violent extremism behind bars and a growing demand for research to identify risk factors and early warning signs of radicalization. While the language of preventive action is often broadly applied to include measures aimed at curbing anti-social behavior, within the field of radicalization studies, early intervention and prevention specifically focus on addressing the processes that lead individuals to adopt extremist beliefs. These initiatives aim to prevent other inmates from being drawn into extremist movements and to stop dangerous extremists from collaborating with each other within the prison environment.

Given the porous nature of some prisons—where information flows in and out, and staff interact with prisoners who may remain connected to their communities—it is also critical to prevent radicalized inmates from maintaining leadership roles within extremist networks. Discussions about de-radicalization often focus on fostering a shift in mindset, encouraging individuals to abandon extremist ideologies. Radicalization is primarily an intra-prison issue, affecting the order and security of prisons, their staff, other inmates, and visitors. However, it also poses external security challenges, as radicalized prisoners may threaten public safety and order upon release. This makes radicalization a long-term concern, as the degree to which governments and agencies address the issue can significantly influence societies' vulnerability to the effects of international terrorism.

Exploring Factors That Contribute To The Process Of Radicalization In Prison

Radicalization in prisons does not follow a single model, as various factors can influence an inmate's path towards extremist ideology at different times and in different ways, creating multiple "entry points." These factors can affect inmates regardless of their personal and ideological backgrounds. Social and psychological factors, such as personality traits and family, social, or group tendencies towards violence, can push inmates towards extremist beliefs. Economic and welfare factors also play a role, as prison communities often face economic disadvantages and marginalization, leading to feelings of dissatisfaction and injustice that can drive radicalization. Additionally, many inmates have criminal backgrounds, blurring the lines between "criminals" and "terrorists."

Radicalization is a relational process, involving the same social mechanisms that foster Jihadist growth outside prison. However, the isolation of imprisonment intensifies these dynamics. Effective prison radicalization models and de-radicalization guidelines must consider these factors, focusing on prevention, post-alert, and defusing strategies. The radicalized inmate is a marginalized figure confronting constitutional freedoms, and prison management might misinterpret religious radicalization as merely a "religious event," especially if the inmate has a history of minor criminal activities. From a criminological perspective, the "normal weight" of such inmates might be quite high.

Assessing And Identifying Radicalized Individuals In Prison

Over the past years, numerous research studies and counter-radicalization strategies have focused on risk assessment and the identification of radicalized individuals. Some projects have developed structured professional assessment tools to evaluate the risk of radicalization and violent intent in prisons, with training programs for these instruments available since 2019. A project, in 2019, documented the success of a conceptual approach to developing another risk-assessment tool. Other studies have created various illustrations for risk assessment tools, establishing links between risk factors and radicalization through investigations or suggesting credible indicators for risk issues that align with certain developmental stages and degrees of radicalization.

However, these strategies face challenges, including the problem of stigmatization effects. Currently, no instrument or diagnostic tool used in preventive risk management in Germany has undergone rigorous evaluation procedures. Trained staff can use a standardized process to decide when to assess potentially radicalized individuals, but to be effective, they must also be trained to conduct these assessments. Given the dynamic nature of radicalization, this should become a required skill for more prison staff over time.

Intervention And Rehabilitation Programs Aim To Support Individuals In Overcoming Challenges And Achieving Long-Term Recovery

In terms of prevention, international literature highlights various intervention programs and rehabilitation projects. Among the best practices in preventing violent extremism are those that go beyond repression, implementing strategies to transition violent extremists back to their state of origin or prepare them for disengagement and reintegration into society. Singapore established a notable rehabilitation project using a three-level model that includes counseling, cognitive-behavioral approaches, and cultural and faith-based programs, yielding positive results. The program's assessment was individualized, focusing on psychiatric advice.

In the Netherlands, an intervention project trained around 15 people in a mosque, providing a place for repentant radicals. A criminologist highlighted both the advantages and disadvantages of this approach, explaining its failure abroad. In Pakistan, 80 religious leaders were hired to reintegrate former prisoners, though the method remains unclear. In Canada, an association collaborated with local agencies to develop a pilot project for gang member reintegration, recruiting 45 participants for training in various aspects, including job placement, mentorship, and weekly individual counseling. Globally, these interventions have had varying levels of success in rehabilitating former radicalized offenders and reintegrating them into society after serving prison time.

Collaborative Strategies For Preventing Radicalization In Prison

This section emphasizes the crucial role of collaboration among internal, external, and multi-stakeholder entities in preventing the spread of radicalization within correctional facilities.

In a conference organized to discuss radicalization among youth in prison, all speakers concurred that prisons alone cannot tackle radicalization effectively. Therefore, partnerships between corrections, governmental agencies, and community organizations are essential, with many adopting a multi-agency approach to create a comprehensive response that spans from prisons to community transition and rehabilitation organizations. The complexity of the issue necessitates collective efforts, as no single stakeholder can address it independently. Additionally, the speakers highlighted that responses to radicalization and violent extremism cannot be implemented economically or efficiently without collaboration. They stressed the importance of using available responses in a complementary manner and overcoming any partnership restrictions.

The value of collaboration in preventing radicalization in prisons is universally acknowledged, as shared resources and stakeholder intelligence lead to more effective interventions. Efforts in prevention and inmate rehabilitation are more efficient and sometimes only possible through partnerships, which are particularly vital for sharing staff training, intervention techniques, and providing a 'client-centered' multi-disciplinary response.

Philanthropic and faith-based approaches were identified as crucial in spreading support and offering alternatives to those vulnerable to radicalization. Many support services for former inmates come from faith-based or non-governmental backgrounds, benefiting from shared values between mentors and clients.

Preventative staff training is also emphasized for its role in creating opportunities to identify at-risk behavior at various stages. Community involvement was also highlighted as essential, with the need for a wide range of community members, who believe in genuine conversation, to support the initiative. This includes working with prisoners' families and former inmates, who often provide valuable intelligence. Effective prevention measures require the integration of internal and external policies and partnerships, balancing these approaches while providing resources for key prevention strategies to ensure a comprehensive and unified response to the threat of extremist radicalization.

CHAPTER 6: WHY DIVORCE AND FAMILY SEPARATION SHOULD BE A LAST RESORT

W e must begin to prioritize reconciliation and explore alternatives to family separation and divorce. Divorce should be a more deliberate and carefully considered decision for those facing marital challenges. Despite rising separation and divorce rates, there is surprisingly little public focus on understanding and addressing these issues effectively. The emotional and practical consequences of divorce are profound, affecting not only the individuals involved but also the broader fabric of society. Yet, decisions to dissolve a marriage are often influenced by misconceptions—such as the fear of professional judgment or concerns about the financial costs of counseling and other efforts to fix the relationship. Additionally, individuals navigating emotionally charged and difficult marital situations may not always approach these decisions with deep reflection. Divorce and separation are life-altering choices with far-reaching implications, from economic and domestic stability to relationships with children.

Historically, the family has been the cornerstone of human development, fostering societal and economic growth. However, many reasons for separation stem from widely circulated misconceptions that often go unexamined and lack scientific scrutiny. Phrases like "divorce hurts families" are generally accepted without question, yet few pause to explore the underlying reasons. This is partly because the instinct to prioritize family integrity—through commitment to marriage and raising children—is no longer deeply ingrained in societal consciousness. Instead, conflicting misconceptions fuel both an eagerness to divorce and staunch opposition to it, creating a landscape of confusion. At the core of these issues lies a pervasive cynicism toward the value of family.

Basic Facts To Know About Divorce And Family Separation

Separation and divorce are both emotional and legal challenges. *Separation* refers to a decision to live apart without formally ending the marriage, while *divorce* is the legal dissolution of a marriage. Both situations can cause significant emotional distress and financial hardship for all involved, especially children, who may face immediate and long-term emotional consequences. While the past cannot be changed, addressing relationship issues early can help prevent separation and divorce.

Because divorce is a legal process, its legal implications often take precedence when relationship problems arise. Divorce has become increasingly common for various reasons, including emotional disconnection or apathy, where individuals "fall out of love" rather than working to maintain their relationship. Societal changes, such as reduced stigma and increased awareness of alternatives, have also influenced divorce rates.

It is crucial for individuals to explore alternatives to divorce before taking such a step. By genuinely attempting to resolve issues, individuals can approach separation or divorce with a clearer conscience if their efforts do not succeed.

The Influence Of Divorce And Family Separation

Divorce and separation are significant life changes that bring emotional, social, and financial challenges. Financial uncertainty often arises as individuals may not fully understand their entitlements or struggle with dividing assets, which can worsen existing issues. Actions or gestures that were once seen positively may take on negative meanings, further complicating the emotional landscape.

These changes can disrupt social connections, reduce exposure to community support, and lead to a loss of contact with extended social networks. Individuals may need to build new support systems while navigating reduced social engagement, particularly when one or both partners withdraw emotionally. Relocating outside the local area adds another layer of complexity, as maintaining contact becomes challenging.

Children often experience similar stressors during a divorce or separation. Research shows that the psychological effects of divorce can persist for more than 25 years, highlighting the long-term impact of such events.

Both men and women face a decline in mental health after divorce, though the reasons differ. Women tend to experience greater economic security post-divorce, especially when they are the ones initiating the separation. This relative stability may help women manage health-related complications more effectively. Men, on the other hand, often experience emotional and economic loss, as they may rely heavily on their wives for emotional support despite generally having better financial positions in society.

Financial issues can further complicate matters, particularly with joint accounts, shared credit, or one partner's financial behaviors impacting the other's credit standing. Separated parties also face increased living costs and income adjustments, which can exacerbate financial stress.

Overall, divorce and separation are multifaceted processes that affect emotional well-being, social stability, and financial security for all involved.

Critical Influence Of Separation And Divorce On Children

When marital problems arise, one of the first concerns is often how they affect the children. Divorce can cause significant emotional distress and stress, making it essential to prioritize their well-being during this challenging time.

The emotional impact on children cannot be overlooked. They often blame themselves for their parents' arguments, unhappiness, or separation. They may experience feelings of stress, powerlessness, sadness, and abandonment. Divorce can also cause confusion, anger, and an overwhelming need to assign blame. Children often fear the loss of one or both parents, which leaves them feeling lonely and afraid. This fear can disrupt their ability to relate well with peers and form intimate relationships. In some cases, children may react by becoming overly self-reliant or acting out in harmful ways. Behaviors such as delinquency, social isolation, estrangement, and anxiety are common when children feel that the family unit is no longer a source of support.

The impact of divorce on children often extends further than expected. Many children of divorced parents struggle with self-doubt, fear of intimacy, and emotional ambivalence in adulthood. Some may unfairly assume parental responsibilities, adding further stress and disrupting their development.

Further considering post-divorce challenges and effects, most children raised by a single parent are often affected emotionally. Research reveals a strong link between marital conflict, divorce, and increased distress in children, which can persist over time. In severe cases, children may experience suicidal thoughts, particularly when parental separation has caused deep emotional wounds.

Our society must ensure that decisions regarding divorce or reconciliation are made with careful consideration, especially when children are involved. It is vital to carefully consider the potential emotional and long-term consequences for children before determining the best course of action. Children can be a good basis for families to stay together; however, if parents decide to remain in an unhappy marriage for their children's sake, it is crucial to work together to resolve issues constructively. This requires all parties to prioritize the family's needs and take deliberate steps toward reconciliation, recognizing the sacrifices both parents and children may endure.

The Impact Of Parental Conflict And Aggression On Children

Several explanations have been proposed to understand how parental conflict and aggression influence children's behavior. Frequent and intense exposure to arguments and hostility can foster impulsive and aggressive problem-solving tendencies in children. While data does not definitively confirm whether conflict primarily leads to aggressive or depressive behaviors, research shows that children exposed to high levels of conflict often struggle with socialization. This association persists even when factors such as economic conditions and parental resources are considered, suggesting that psychological mechanisms—like low self-esteem—play a significant role in children's reactions to conflict.

Studies have also found a strong correlation between parental conflict and youth criminality. The more severe and violent the conflict, the higher the likelihood of delinquent behavior in children. For instance, research on fifth graders in public elementary schools revealed that violence at home, combined with exposure to violent neighborhoods, significantly increases the risk of youth delinquency. This connection between domestic violence and antisocial behavior has been observed in both children and adults, with one two-year study of over 1,700 adults linking constant parental conflict to higher levels of mental distress in adulthood.

Children raised in homes with unresolved and hostile interactions often internalize violence as a normal response to conflict, which can negatively affect their adult relationships and friendships. Studies have shown that elementary and middle school children are more likely to view hitting or fighting as acceptable if they regularly witness such behaviors at home. Over time, these children are at increased risk of adopting aggressive behavior patterns themselves. Teaching children conflict resolution, emotional regulation, and social skills can mitigate these tendencies, but traumatized children often miss these critical socialization opportunities.

In households marked by high conflict, parents may cope by becoming overly permissive, avoiding discipline, or placating their children through bribes and special treats to minimize further tension. Such parenting approaches, while understandable, can reinforce negative behaviors in children.

The consequences of domestic violence are not limited to observing physical aggression. Children who *hear* but do not *see* violence are at even greater risk of becoming violent themselves. Moreover, child abuse often coincides with exposure to emotional and physical violence, exacerbating the trauma. Encouragingly, studies have shown that mothers who are aware of their children's exposure to domestic violence often respond with heightened protective behaviors and concern for their well-being.

To improve outcomes for children affected by parental conflict, it is crucial to address violence as a systemic family issue. While divorce can exacerbate these challenges, understanding what makes it particularly problematic for children—and addressing their needs— can foster better outcomes for children between the ages of 7 to 13 and future generations.

How Divorce And Family Separation Increase Criminality Among Children

Divorce rates are widespread globally, with approximately one-third of marriages in the United States ending in legal separation. This figure increases further when considering couples who choose to part ways before finalizing a legal divorce. These separations and divorces are often linked to negative consequences for child development, education, and criminal behavior.

The effects of divorce are multifaceted, leading to significant losses for both parents and children. These include reduced investments in human capital, emotional distress, instability, social stigma, and increased exposure to conflict. Children may witness or experience violence, endure compensated or broken home dynamics, and develop behavioral issues in response to these challenges. Research indicates that nearly one-quarter of children from these families experience physical abuse or sexual molestation, while nearly half engage in violence toward their parents. However, the relationship between divorce and criminality is complex rather than straightforward. For instance, adolescents are generally less likely than younger children to commit intimate violence or act aggressively toward their parents.

While divorce damages children's development and stability, this does not always translate directly into criminal behavior. Instead, the disruption may foster complex reactive strategies, such as delinquency, income-seeking behaviors, or violence, though the connection remains unclear. Regardless of the specific empirical evidence supporting these theories, it is evident that inequalities resulting from family disruptions must be examined to fully understand the broader complications and consequences that arise from divorce.

Criminality Traits Acquired Through Observing

Social Learning Theory suggests that children acquire behaviors and attitudes by observing and imitating those around them, particularly significant role models such as parents. Consequently, children exposed to aggressive or violent parental behaviors are more likely to replicate those actions. Parents, as primary role models, influence how individuals perceive and implement conflict resolution strategies. These models of behavior not only shape children's understanding of aggression but also teach potential methods for managing conflicts, often rooted in aggression as a response to personal attacks.

According to Social Learning Theory, exposure to emotional and physical aggression within the family unit teaches individuals that violence can be rationalized and justified. This rationale normalizes aggressive responses, leading members of society to view such behaviors as acceptable in similar circumstances. Repeated exposure to severe, persistent family violence can condition individuals to perceive such aggression as a legitimate form of conflict resolution, reinforcing dangerous interpretations of direct aggression.

In violent households, a conditioned response often emerges during acts of family violence. Perpetrators impulsively shift blame onto the victim, rationalizing their violent behaviors as a reaction to something the victim allegedly did wrong. This victim-blaming narrative serves to justify and excuse the use of violence. Over time, repeated exposure to these violent interactions can desensitize observers to the severity of the aggression. As a result, individuals may not only attach value to such behaviors but may also feel encouraged to imitate them.

Empirical evidence consistently demonstrates that children from violent or abusive households are more likely to exhibit violent behaviors themselves. In contrast, children from low-violence or non-violent families are less inclined to resort to physical force, particularly as an initial response to conflict. Observing domestic violence is a strong predictor of future violent behavior, particularly the intent to engage in aggression against women during adulthood. For example, exposure to persistent maternal battering during childhood can condition boys to accept or minimize the seriousness of adult male aggression.

Research highlights the critical impact of early exposure to familial violence on future behavior. Children who witness violence are more likely to internalize these patterns and perpetuate them, contributing to a cycle of aggression that can persist into adulthood.

Contributory Factors That Increase Crime In Our Society

Several factors contribute to criminal behavior among children, including stress, emotional distress, and aggression as a coping mechanism for frustration and tension. These factors help explain why many —but not all—children from divorced or separated families may develop criminal tendencies. Research links family conflict to a rise in behavioral and emotional challenges in children, such as ADHD-like symptoms, task avoidance, aggression, psychosomatic complaints, academic anxiety (e.g., fear of the blackboard or numbers), sleep disturbances, and overall emotional distress.

The relationship between inter-parental conflicts and childhood emotional distress is deeply influenced by how children perceive their parents' arguments and relate them to their own experiences. A child's interpretation of parental aggression strongly predicts externalized symptoms, such as behavioral issues, following a divorce. Numerous studies have found a correlation between frequent parental aggression and diminished emotional resilience in children, which contributes to mental health challenges during childhood and adolescence and, in some cases, leads to criminal behavior.

The documented outcomes of parental aggression on children include externalized behavioral symptoms, emotional distress, and the internalization of conflict dynamics. However, additional external factors also play a role in delinquency. The social repercussions of having divorced or separated parents include changing neighborhoods, reduced household income, the need to use parental cash for tasks previously supported by parental time, adapting to a parent's dating life, and navigating relationships with step siblings.

In practice, peer group behavior often has a stronger influence on delinquency than family dynamics. The need for offenders to avoid isolation in their deviant behavior has long been recognized as a driving factor in delinquency. Economic theories of crime also highlight the role of social solidarity and reference groups in shaping decision-making, including the perceived risks of criminal activity.

The emotional trauma of parental divorce or separation often spills over into both actions and feelings, a phenomenon referred to here as *emotional spillover*. Borrowed from economic terminology, this concept describes the negative emotional impacts caused by the transfer of risks and stresses from one domain to another. In this context, the psychic trauma experienced by children translates into behavioral and emotional consequences that can contribute to criminal behavior.

Substance Abuse And Risky Behaviors

Children of divorced parents are at an increased risk of engaging in substance abuse and other risky behaviors. The likelihood of drug use rises significantly when a child experiences multiple family separations, as the instability weakens the foundation for sound decision-making. Statistics show that 25% of children from divorced families use drugs, with similar rates among children living with single parents and even higher rates for those with stepparents. Beyond drug use, children from broken families are more likely to engage in delinquent behavior, early sexual activity, unintended pregnancies, and other risky actions. These behaviors often correlate with poor academic performance, reduced educational opportunities, and a higher likelihood of dropping out of school.

The reasons behind these risky behaviors vary but often include coping with emotional distress. Many children turn to drugs or risky activities to escape the discomfort of pain caused by family instability. Adverse childhood experiences, such as witnessing family conflict or experiencing neglect, significantly increase the likelihood of smoking, experimenting with drugs, and substance dependency. These behaviors also increase the risk of mental health challenges, including anxiety, depression, and self-harm, often perpetuating a cycle of self-sabotage.

Preventing these outcomes requires early intervention

and the creation of supportive, stable environments. Programs designed to address risk and protective factors for adolescents—especially in calm, nurturing communities—can help mitigate long-term consequences. Additionally, peer influence plays a critical role in shaping behaviors, making community-based prevention efforts essential. Efforts to combat substance abuse should also include initiatives to support postnatal women with high-risk substance use disorders, improve access to care, and reduce stigma. Comprehensive strategies that address the root causes of these behaviors can provide sustainable solutions and improve the well-being of affected children and families.

Emotional Distress And Mental Health Consequences Of Divorce Or Separation

Divorce and separation can have both immediate and long-term effects on mental health. Individuals facing challenges across physical, social, legal, and financial dimensions often struggle to manage the stress associated with these life changes. This can increase the likelihood of mental health issues.

Emotional stress and anger are common, as they are part of the grief cycle that accompany such transitions. Many individuals feel isolated throughout the mediation, legal, or trial processes, and these feelings are often exacerbated by the fear of financial instability or losing custody of their children. Such fears contribute to intense emotions like betrayal, sadness, hopelessness, and loss.

Decades of research demonstrate that children often experience profound emotional disturbances following family separation, with increased risks of depression, anxiety, behavioral difficulties, and substance use. Emotional distress is a well-documented factor in criminal offending, yet less attention has been given to children who develop behavioral issues as a result. Many children initially respond to parental divorce or separation with emotional difficulties, but a smaller subgroup adopts maladaptive coping strategies, such as substance use, to alleviate their distress. This behavior further impacts their emotional well-being and increases their likelihood of engaging in delinquent or criminal activities. Extensive studies have established substance use as a mediator in the relationship between parental divorce and delinquency.

A child's ability to cope with the trauma of family separation is closely tied to the family's capacity to provide care and structure after the event. Children exposed to neglect, abuse, or ongoing parental conflict are at heightened risk of developing externalizing behaviors, as they lack respite from the turmoil. While evidence suggests that some effects of family separation may be transient, emerging research highlights the long-term consequences for children who are not adequately supported during these adverse experiences. Mental health disturbances resulting from family separation significantly increase the risk of criminal behavior, underscoring the importance of interventions that address both the immediate and long-term impacts on children. Understanding these pathways is critical for developing targeted strategies to mitigate the behavioral and emotional consequences of family separation.

At any stage of the separation or divorce process, it is essential to encourage individuals to explore their options and seek support. Providing educational resources, encouraging them to talk with others who have navigated similar challenges, and recommending professional mental health evaluations are key steps to managing emotional stress.

Working with an experienced professional can help individuals and families cope with the emotional turmoil that arises when a once-stable life faces upheaval. These experts can provide tailored strategies for navigating the emotional "storm" and help rebuild a sense of stability and hope for the future.

Preventive Measures And Interventions: Mitigating The Impact Of Divorce On Children

Preventive measures are crucial to minimize the negative effects of divorce or separation on children and prevent the manifestation of behavioral or emotional problems. These strategies include promoting co-parenting through parental support programs, offering couples counseling before conflicts escalate, providing safe and neutral spaces for child exchanges in high-conflict situations, and enforcing agreements with minimal disputes.

Recognizing the significant impact of divorce, authorities in the Netherlands have shifted from reactive to preventive approaches, combining multi-faceted interventions informed by European institutions and scientific research. While these measures are most effective when implemented early, they can still yield positive outcomes years after a separation. Special attention is given to vulnerable groups, including adolescent boys in care facilities, to address their unique needs. Carefully evaluating awareness campaigns, breaking harmful silences, and expanding successful strategies are essential for improving the well-being of children affected by parental separation. Coordinated efforts, backed by evidence-based guidance and resources, play a vital role in ensuring better outcomes for these children.

Reconciliation As An Option

Spouses should remember that reconciliation is always a possible path forward. Before pursuing divorce or permanent separation, individuals must thoroughly evaluate the physical, mental, legal, financial, and social consequences of their decision. Notably, the potential benefits of reconciliation often set the highest benchmark for comparison when considering legal dissolution.

Highlighting the impact of stress on mental and emotional well-being is not meant to discourage individuals from considering separation or divorce. Rather, it underscores the importance of addressing mental and communication conflicts constructively. Resolving these issues—whether during reconciliation or beyond—can help minimize the negative effects on everyone's mental health. Professional counseling is strongly recommended, as trained experts can guide spouses and families through the challenges of managing stress as both partners and parents.

The Financial Impact Of Divorce And Separation

Nearly all individuals who experience divorce or separation face significant, and often long-lasting, financial strain. One of the primary concerns in divorce proceedings is the division of assets accumulated during the marriage. Financial decisions during this time often focus on how to disentangle obligations that were originally based on maintaining a shared lifestyle. These issues are usually among the first—and most complex—topics to address.

When children are involved, financial concerns expand beyond asset division to include child-related expenses. Child support and parenting arrangements are central considerations. Child support laws ensure that financial responsibilities for children remain fair and consistent, regardless of the family's circumstances.

Spousal support, while historically common for wives, is now available to either spouse. Its purpose is to minimize financial hardship for the lower-earning spouse after the divorce. A spouse may receive support if they lack the earning capacity to maintain the lifestyle they had during the marriage. This is particularly relevant when one partner made economic sacrifices—such as prioritizing childcare or supporting their spouse's career—at the expense of their own earning potential.

The economic fallout from divorce, including both immediate and long-term income loss, can exacerbate financial challenges. While custody-related costs may decline over time, financial issues often remain unresolved. In many cases, divorce shifts financial problems rather than solving them.

Preventing Greater Financial Instability

To minimize financial hardship, divorcing spouses are encouraged to explore all available options, including legal support, divorce mediation, or commercial solutions to address financial needs. In some cases, reconciliation may present a viable alternative to further financial decline, especially when couples can address and resolve underlying disagreements.

Ultimately, financial well-being and marital harmony are closely linked. A thoughtful and strategic approach to financial matters during divorce can help mitigate the risk of prolonged financial instability.

Reconciliation As A First Step

Many couples fail to realize that divorce or separation doesn't have to be their first or only option; instead, they can choose to take a step toward reconciliation.

Relationships are inherently challenging, and many couples find themselves contemplating separation simply because they have never engaged in open, honest, and meaningful conversations about the root causes of their dissatisfaction. Such conversations—whether a single dialogue or a series—can often dispel long-held fears about their relationship. These discussions offer a path to healing, moving forward together, or making a more informed decision about the future.

However, after years—or even decades—of shared experiences, disagreements, and emotional pain, it is natural for couples to feel disconnected or misunderstood. Many struggling couples may therefore lack the foundation of trust needed to address the root causes of their dissatisfaction. This is where counseling, coaching, or therapy becomes invaluable. Trained professionals can facilitate these conversations, guiding partners to communicate constructively and equipping them with tools to rebuild their connection.

Unresolved hurt, anger, bitterness, infidelity, addiction, financial strain, and ongoing disagreements are all valid reasons for couples to feel unsure about their future. However, counseling or therapy offers practical solutions to work through these struggles, encouraging couples to persevere through difficult times. Decisions about whether to stay together or part ways should be grounded in understanding—not avoidance, assumptions, or emotional certainty.

Reconciliation is worth exploring, even when a relationship feels irreparably damaged. Progress may have stalled, the root causes of pain may be unclear, or unresolved questions may linger—such as, "Why are we so angry with each other?" When relationships falter, the path forward often begins with introspection—looking inwards. Through open, guided, and transformative conversations, couples can find clarity and meaning.

Ultimately, seeking reconciliation allows couples to confront their struggles head-on and determine whether their relationship can be revived or if separation is the best choice. Either way, the process provides understanding, healing, and a clearer path forward.

Counseling And Therapy

The first step toward reconciliation, before anything else is considered, is engaging individuals or couples in counseling or therapy. Therapy provides a safe space for partners to openly express their differences and work toward understanding. Guided by a professional, the process offers support and expert direction, allowing the therapist to identify damaging relational patterns and provide guidance on restructuring them. Therapy serves as a dedicated platform for couples to unpack emotions and mindsets surrounding divorce, separation, or reconciliation. While these sessions can be emotionally intense and sometimes frustrating, they offer an opportunity to address underlying issues in a structured way.

There are instances where therapy sessions bring deeply held emotions and past mistakes to the surface. In one case, the wife left home immediately after a particularly emotional session. However, through continued communication and reconciliation efforts, she eventually returned, and the relationship improved. This example highlights that while therapy can present challenges, it also equips couples with the tools for growth and healing when handled with commitment and care.

Ultimately, therapy is about working through a relationship's difficulties and improving it. These sessions allow couples to explore concepts and emotions that may not surface as easily in individual settings. However, success in therapy requires a willingness to put in the effort and navigate the process safely. Partners must remain committed and not abandon the process simply because they encounter a difficult moment.

The benefits of therapy include helping individuals and couples identify and learn new strategies to cope with the emotional challenges of reconciliation or separation. Most therapy protocols provide concrete, actionable strategies to bridge emotional gaps and rebuild connections. With dedication, therapy can help couples reconcile or, at the very least, gain clarity and closure about their relationship.

Embracing Alternatives To Divorce

Couples contemplating separation or divorce have several options to consider. If couples are uncertain about ending their relationship and find themselves at an impasse, they can choose to explore whether it can be saved.

Mediation is one option, offering a cooperative and creative approach to problem-solving that empowers couples to resolve disputes in a respectful and lasting manner. Another option is legal separation, where couples request the courts to allow them to live apart while remaining legally married. For some, this arrangement ensures the continuation of certain benefits, such as shared medical insurance, especially if finances are a concern. For others, it provides a transitional period to adjust and plan the next steps in their lives. Trial separation is another commonly chosen path. In this scenario, couples agree to live separately for a defined or flexible period, giving them time to reflect on what they want from the relationship. During this time, they may choose to work with a therapist or other professionals to gain insight into their individual needs, wishes, and unresolved conflicts. Trial separation also creates an opportunity for reconciliation, particularly for those who may not have previously recognized the underlying issues in their marriage.

When couples enter the formal divorce process, it is often because at least one partner has made a firm decision to leave the relationship. In some cases, a spouse may proceed with a legal divorce even if they are unsure about the decision, skipping the time needed to fully consider or grieve the loss. This can lead to lingering, unresolved feelings of sadness, hurt, or anger that may not align with the finality of their decision.

GBENGA ANOLA

CHAPTER 7: THE PARENTS' ROLE: BRIDGING MENTAL HEALTH, EDUCATION, AND LAW ENFORCEMENT

The relationship between parents, mental health institutions, schools, and law enforcement is vital for ensuring the well-being and safety of children, especially those struggling with mental health challenges. Parents play a critical role in bridging these systems, facilitating communication, and ensuring proper coordination. Students battling depression or mental disorders are often at risk of unpredictable behavior, which may lead to criminal activities. Schools must be aware of these students' mental health conditions to enable effective collaboration with mental health institutions. This coordination ensures that students receive appropriate care and treatment while being closely monitored to prevent harm to themselves or others. An area of particular concern is the issuance of gun licenses to individuals with mental or psychological disorders. For the safety of society, this issue must be thoroughly addressed through stringent evaluations and oversight mechanisms.

Mental health services, educational institutions, and law enforcement each play distinct yet interconnected roles. Mental health services focus on the emotional and psychological well-being of children, while schools prioritize student learning and development. Police, on the other hand, often encounter mental health issues in the context of crime and disorder, and are frequently the first point of contact for families in crisis. A robust network of support services is therefore essential for effectively addressing these challenges, and the success of these relationships significantly impacts the opportunities available to children, particularly those in difficult circumstances. Such a network must be built on mutual respect and a clear understanding of the unique objectives and responsibilities of each profession. By fostering open communication and collaborative efforts, parents can play an invaluable role in creating a framework that complements institutional support and promotes the overall development and safety of children and youth.

The Relevance And Significance Of Family Values To Society

The tragic story of Seung-Hui Cho highlights several critical factors that deserve deeper examination. Cho was affected by a range of risk factors, particularly social ones, such as poverty, limited resources, associations with antisocial peers, and peer rejection. Reports indicate he was frequently bullied by other children, including those from affluent backgrounds at his church. These experiences likely fueled his antisocial behavior, which may have eventually escalated into criminal actions.

Nikki Giovanni, one of Cho's professors, described him as mean-spirited and a bully. The English department faculty expressed concerns about his behavior, and Lucinda Roy, co-director of the school's creative writing program, even removed him from class, tutored him individually, and urged him to seek counseling. Despite these interventions, Cho was still able to legally purchase firearms. Reports show he bought his first handgun five weeks before his mass shooting, which remains one of the deadliest school shootings in U.S. history, followed by the acquisition of a second firearm closer to the event.

This raises pressing questions about gun regulations. Stricter controls should have been implemented long ago, yet debates on the issue continue. When individuals who have endured significant societal setbacks can easily access firearms, the risks of mass violence increase. Who will be the next victim, and where will the next shooting occur?

Additionally, the report suggests Cho exhibited symptoms of depressive disorder. Persistent depression can lead to suicidal tendencies, and in some cases, acts of violence like mass shootings. This tragic case underscores the urgent need for comprehensive mental health support and stricter gun control measures.

Today's youth face a wide range of mental health challenges, affecting students across all educational levels, from young children to college undergraduates. At least 25% of college students report experiencing mental health concerns, which, if left unaddressed, can have long-lasting impacts on their overall well-being. At the primary and secondary school levels, incidents such as school shootings have prompted various responses, including proposals to arm teachers, calls for greater involvement of mental health professionals, and discussions about removing police from school campuses.

The presence of police in schools can positively impact school safety, acting as both a deterrent and a partner in emergency and disaster response. Police are often called upon to manage students who behave in ways that deviate from the norm, including those experiencing mental health crises. In recent years, law enforcement has responded to school shootings, frequently disarming attackers and preventing further harm. However, while schools need help coordinating services for students with mental health needs, systemic barriers often result in the exclusion of police from conversations about mental health interventions. Additionally, police have sometimes used force against disruptive students as young as six years old on school campuses, highlighting a significant issue within the system that cannot be ignored. There has been minimal legislative effort to reduce the use of force on young students, especially those with mental health or special education needs. This situation reflects a broader culture within schools that prioritizes rule-following and safety, often at the expense of addressing mental health concerns. Critics argue that the focus on safety, rather than security, should lead to a reevaluation of the use of force against youth. Chronic punitive measures, including the use of force, have long-term negative effects on children and do not address the root causes of their behaviors.

Mental health professionals play a crucial role in schools, with ample evidence showing that students who receive mental health services improve and achieve better outcomes. With proper resources and training, mental health therapists can intervene in real-time to de-escalate situations without resorting to psychiatric facility admissions or police involvement. Given the logistical challenges of expanding mental health services in the U.S., partnerships between schools and law enforcement can increase the support available to students in crisis. Schools are not shirking their responsibility to educational success by involving the police. In fact, the best outcomes for children can be achieved through collaborative efforts between schools, law enforcement, and mental health professionals.

Prevalence Of Mental Health In Schools

Statistics show that 1 in 5 children and adolescents are significantly affected by mental illness, highlighting the broad spectrum of mental health disorders among young people. For instance, anxiety disorders have a 12-month prevalence of 7.1% among children aged 6-17, while 13.3% of adolescents aged 13-18 experience major depression within the same period. Additionally, post-traumatic stress disorder affects 3.8% of children aged 3-6 and 5% of youth aged 7-18. Tragically, suicide is the second leading cause of death among children aged 10-14. These statistics highlight the serious and varied nature of mental health challenges faced by youth.

Other significant statistics include the fact that up to 25% of students may struggle with a mental health disorder in any given year, while social and emotional issues disrupt learning for approximately 10 million students. Furthermore, suicide is the third leading cause of death for individuals aged 15-24 and the sixth leading cause for those aged 5-14. These figures emphasize the urgent need for proper mental health services for students, a need that has only recently gained the attention it deserves through research. However, it's important to note that these statistics are based on data that is now over eight years old, underscoring the need for updated information and ongoing support for mental health in educational settings.

Mental health is a significant issue in schools, not only because it affects the safety and well-being of students and staff but also because it plays a crucial role in academic success. It is estimated that out of 13-20% of children and adolescents who will experience a mental health concern, only 25% receive support through an individualized education plan (IEP) within the school setting. The prevalence of mental health issues increases as children grow older, with emotional and behavioral problems affecting 20-25% of high school students. Disturbingly, 78% of school-aged children with emotional or behavioral issues do not receive support from mental health professionals outside of the school system.

Students with mental health issues, such as anxiety and depression, are 2.5 to 3 times more likely to face learning difficulties and are more likely to be classified for special education. These students are also 5 to 6 times more likely to drop out of school compared to their peers without emotional or behavioral problems. Furthermore, students with anxiety are more likely to repeat a grade. Research indicates that 20-25% of elementary school students exhibit at least two anxiety symptoms, while 25-50% of middle school students who struggle with anxiety end up repeating a grade. Mental health problems can also result in externalizing behaviors like bullying, fighting, and truancy, or internalizing behaviors like withdrawal, all of which disrupt the school environment.

Within the classroom, students with mental health diagnoses often require additional assistance, disrupt activities, or fail to respond to consequences. Their peers are more likely to reject them as friends, further isolating these students and exacerbating the problem. Students with emotional and behavioral issues are also more likely to be suspended, with half of those exhibiting externalizing behaviors being suspended at least once before the age of 13, twice the rate of their peers without behavioral problems.

To address these challenges, schools have placed a strong emphasis on mental health promotion, early intervention, and prevention policies. Several intervention programs focus on early intervention for younger children, participation in competitive sports, and post-disaster mental health support both in and out of the classroom. Combating stigma, launching educational campaigns about mental health, and assessing the mental health of teachers and school staff are also key strategies for improving the school environment. Additionally, many professional organizations for educators have developed teaching standards that promote inclusivity and sensitivity toward students with mental health issues, fostering a positive and supportive classroom climate.

In summary, mental health is a critical consideration in schools, supported by extensive research, highlighting the need for continued attention and intervention.

Overcoming Stigma And Addressing Misconceptions

Public stigma surrounding mental health often results in discrimination against a diverse range of individuals. Despite communities' opposition to profiling and restrictive policies, addressing this stigma requires a politically sensitive but crucial effort: re-educating the public based on data and facts about the prevalence, treatment, and success rates of mental health interventions. Unfortunately, the treatment process for individuals with mental illness can sometimes feel dehumanizing, and the stigma extends not only to those experiencing mental health issues but also to the professionals involved in their care. Mental health personnel, educators, and law enforcement officers often become targets of this stigma, as they are perceived by some as part of the problem when treatment outcomes fail or lead to incarceration.

Professionals frequently express frustration with the persistent challenges they face when working with families affected by mental illness. Both school and law enforcement personnel often rely on control-based methods to address behavioral issues, but these approaches are typically ineffective and can exacerbate negative attitudes. Without proactive efforts by professionals to educate the public— through media outreach or community engagement— misunderstandings and stigma will persist, hindering the acceptance of mental health services.

For parents, combating stigma involves fostering open conversations about mental health and encouraging the use of mental health services without shame or fear of judgment. By addressing misconceptions and modeling acceptance, parents can promote positive attitudes toward mental health care among children, adolescents, and young adults. This modeling is critical to developing help-seeking behaviors in youth and cultivating a culture of acceptance. Parents can further contribute by sharing their own positive experiences with mental health practitioners, demonstrating tolerance for diversity, and advocating for mental health awareness in their communities.

Building trust between mental health providers, schools, and communities is essential to reducing stigma and fostering collaboration. Trust relies on faith in the integrity, consistency, and transparency of actions and communication. Research suggests that trust in administrative systems is strongly linked to positive outcomes, making it vital to eliminate misunderstandings, rumors, and misinformation that undermine service providers. However, stigma and limited resources remain significant barriers to effective collaboration. Overcoming these challenges requires a unified effort to educate, build trust, and promote acceptance, paving the way for better outcomes for individuals and communities alike.

Obstacles And Challenges In Building Effective Collaboration

Research highlights numerous obstacles and challenges to effective collaboration between schools, police, and mental health services, many of which stem from systemic issues. Each sector operates under distinct legislation and guidelines, which can lead to misunderstandings and misalignments. Funding limitations further hinder service provision, while professionals may perceive other sectors as overly rigid or inflexible compared to their own. Additionally, unclear communication structures, the absence of established guidelines, and insufficient cross-sector training often delay service delivery and lead to underutilized resources. Many professionals also lack a full understanding of what other sectors can contribute, which exacerbates these issues.

Discrepancies in roles and objectives can also disrupt collaboration. Without clearly defined goals, initiatives often lose direction. Training resources are typically siloed, catering separately to educators, mental health workers, or police, without a unified resource encompassing all three sectors. This fragmented approach contributes to hierarchical dynamics, particularly between police and mental health professionals. Police, often acting as gatekeepers of safety, operate within bureaucratic and paramilitary cultures that may conflict with the approaches of schools and mental health services.

In disadvantaged communities, schools are sometimes marginalized, especially during emergencies or disasters. As primary responders, police often dominate resource allocation, sidelining school and mental health needs. For instance, after a major disaster, rebuilding schools was delayed as other priorities took precedence. This underscores how professional priorities and identities can overshadow urgent concerns, such as deciding whether police or mental health teams should respond to a psychiatric emergency.

Parent advocacy plays a crucial role in ensuring students' needs are prioritized. When parents lack awareness or support to advocate effectively, conflicts can arise within the community. Strengthening ongoing relationships between school counselors, police, and other services can streamline future processes, reducing reliance on crisis-driven responses. Teachers have emphasized the importance of pre-planned, mutually understood procedures among counselors, police, and mental health workers. Such planning clarifies roles, ensures appropriate backup, and fosters a more collaborative and effective approach to addressing challenges.

Parents As Key Connectors In Bridging The Gap

Parents play a pivotal role in bridging the gap between mental health, education, and criminal justice systems. Beyond advocating for their child's needs, parents act as essential connectors by participating in discussions and decision-making processes with mental health clinicians, educators, and law enforcement. These interactions help break down information silos across sectors and foster better collaboration. Effective communication strategies include active listening, building trust and rapport, staying open to input and assistance, following clear guidelines, and advocating with respect and understanding. Parents can engage more effectively by recognizing the unique roles, language, and priorities of each sector, as well as the dynamics of power distribution within these systems.

Parents bring invaluable insights, drawing on their personal knowledge of their child and their experiences navigating various services. They often connect the "dots" that professionals might overlook, offering a broader understanding of the child's needs, the community, and societal challenges. While services may sometimes fall short of parents' expectations, this gap often stems from a misalignment between what is offered and what is truly needed. By engaging with parents, professionals can gain a deeper understanding of these shortcomings and work collaboratively to improve policies and practices.

Open dialogue with parents not only enhances service delivery but also fosters a shared vision among professionals and families. Empowering parents with firsthand knowledge of available services, laws, policies, and practices, and equipping them with advocacy and navigation skills, strengthens their ability to support their children. It's important to recognize that parents are often the most consistent presence in a child's life over the long term. Their determination and resilience are critical assets that services and professionals should support and harness to ensure sustained and meaningful collaboration. And it also becomes imperative that parents should step up to the challenge knowing fully well that they often become the next target of attack.

Looking critically at the case of Christopher Porco, a 21-year-old who had a strained relationship with his parents, we see a troubling series of events. Christopher exhibited behaviors often associated with psychopathy, which culminated in a tragic and violent crime. Despite their difficulties, his parents expressed unconditional love and concern for his future. Even after Christopher forged his father's signature to co-sign a loan without his knowledge, his father spoke on behalf of himself and his wife, affirming their love for their son. Tragically, just two weeks later, Christopher murdered his father, Peter Porco. He broke into their home, disabled the burglar alarm, and attacked his father with an ax. This calculated act highlights traits associated with psychopathy, such as impulsivity and a lack of empathy. Psychopaths often hastily plan or spontaneously engage in serious crimes for immediate gratification, unlike professional criminals who act with purpose and a clear plan.

Christopher's behavior also reflected other psychopathic tendencies, such as externalizing blame. After being forced to withdraw from the University of Rochester in Fall 2003 due to failing grades, he falsely claimed that a professor had lost his final exam instead of accepting responsibility.

Although Christopher has not been formally diagnosed

as a psychopath, his actions and behaviors exhibit many characteristics of the condition. Ultimately, he was convicted and sentenced to 50 years in prison but continues to adamantly assert his innocence. This case underscores the complex interplay of personality traits, family dynamics, and criminal behavior.

Key Strategies And Best Practices For Successful Collaboration

Research has identified several successful strategies to enhance collaboration between services, focusing on mutual trust, information sharing, and regular communication. A key best practice is to designate a leader with the authority to organize regular meetings with representatives from all involved agencies, which helps to address the animosity and mistrust that may exist between professionals. These meetings should be structured to facilitate open dialogue and cooperation. Training programs that involve staff from police, mental health services, and schools have been shown to be particularly effective in promoting interagency collaboration, as they encourage mutual understanding and shared goals.

Joint meetings, where staff from various sectors such as the police, mental health services, and schools come together, have proven successful in fostering improved relationships and pooling resources and ideas. Holding these meetings in venues where schools already meet can be particularly effective. The presence of police staff is often viewed as providing external authority and balance, which can be especially helpful in complex cases that require broader perspectives or deeper systemic engagement. Including parents in these training sessions and multi-agency initiatives is also crucial, as parents are experts on their children and bring valuable insights to the table. By addressing parents' concerns about accessing services across different agencies and working together to find solutions, the collaboration can be more effective and inclusive.

To ensure positive interactions between sectors, interagency protocols and procedures should be established. These protocols should outline the process for sharing information, with clear consent and permission forms, ensuring that families are informed about who will receive what information. These practices were developed as part of an independent evaluation of a partnerships project aimed at improving collaboration.

Case studies of successful collaboration between schools, children's mental health services, and police highlight the benefits of a coordinated approach. For example, delivering mental health training to teachers and school staff helps ensure consistent communication and collaboration between schools and mental health services. This training also empowers headteachers and governors to play a key role in identifying and promoting good practices. Parent participation is also another essential element of successful collaboration. Including parents in needs-definition and service planning groups ensures that their perspectives are considered and that they can actively contribute to shaping services.

Literature consistently emphasizes that one-time information sessions or training cannot achieve the necessary attitudinal or behavioral changes. It is also crucial for schools and mental health services to have an upfront, agreed-upon understanding regarding confidential information sharing with police when appropriate, ensuring that collaboration is both effective and respectful of privacy.

Educational And Training Initiatives

Training and education programs focused on effective collaboration should be provided to frontline staff across multiple sectors, including mental health organizations, schools and school boards, court systems, local law enforcement, and relevant social service agencies. These programs must be tailored to the specific needs of each sector while being rooted in evidence-based practices that frequently engage children and families. The training should address each sector's mandates, priorities, and imperatives, while equipping participants with essential skills in crisis intervention, mental health awareness, and communication strategies.

Parents should also be included in these educational initiatives, as they play a crucial role in advocating for their children and families when accessing services. These programs will empower parents with the knowledge and tools to better navigate the system and support their children's needs. Once these programs are established, it is important to continue ongoing education to keep up with new research, evolving best practices, and changing local needs.

In addition to training for first responders and frontline support staff, it is essential to provide interdisciplinary training for supervisors and managers who oversee these staff members. The complexities of managing interagency collaboration often tie into the broader organizational goals and 'bottom lines' of each agency. Although these initiatives require significant investment, the long-term benefits for children, youth, families, and communities are substantial. Strengthening collaboration through comprehensive training helps improve the quality of life in communities and enhances the effectiveness of services provided to children, their families, and the professionals who support them.

GBENGA ANOLA

CHAPTER 8: GOD'S ROLE IN FAMILY GUIDANCE AND SECURITY

We cannot disregard God's position as the Creator and Architect of the human race. According to His divine plan, the family is central to His purpose for humanity. This truth is evident in the Word of God, as seen in Genesis 1:28 where He commands humanity to "be fruitful and multiply, replenish the earth, and subdue it, and have dominion over every living thing." This verse underscores the importance of the family in fulfilling God's plan for mankind.

Three key directives from Genesis 1:28 are particularly relevant to addressing the challenges faced by families and society today: "be fruitful and multiply," "replenish the earth," and "subdue it."

The command to "be fruitful and multiply" emphasizes procreation and the growth of humanity. However, being fruitful extends beyond bearing children; it encompasses productivity and the cultivation of life, which includes intentionally fostering good qualities in others. Many couples misinterpret this command, focusing solely on abundance while neglecting their responsibility to nurture and develop life. Cultivation, whether improving relationships, skills, or character, is integral to fulfilling this command, especially in parenting.

The phrase "replenish the earth" is sometimes misunderstood as "refill," but the Hebrew word *mala* means "to fill" or "to fulfill." This directive calls for populating the earth and realizing its full potential. Similarly, the command to "subdue" the earth conveys humanity's responsibility to manage and utilize the earth's resources wisely. Subduing does not imply exploitation but rather stewardship—ensuring sustainability while benefiting from these resources.

Our responsibility to steward the earth begins with the family, the foundation of society. While challenges are inevitable, we must rise to meet them to fulfill God's purpose for humanity. In this context, God's command to "have dominion" places us in a unique position to oversee and maintain the balance of the natural world. Together, these commands outline humanity's role in managing all that happens on earth, starting with the family.

We cannot remain passive observers in the face of challenges, as doing so would undermine God's plan for humanity. In John 11:38-44, when Jesus raised Lazarus, He instructed the people to roll away the stone before performing the miracle. This demonstrates the necessity of human effort in partnership with divine intervention. Just as the people removed the stone, we must actively labor in God's plan while trusting Him to do what we cannot do.

The family is the starting point for creating a better world. The Bible teaches us to "train up a child in the way he should go, and when he is old, he will not depart from it" (Proverbs 22:6). While parenting can be challenging, much like an apprentice learning a new skill, persistence and prayer can lead to success. Children may not grasp everything immediately, but with patience and guidance, they will grow into the values instilled in them.

This book is not just a collection of ideas—it is a movement. If every married individual embraces its principles, we can raise a generation rooted in peace and integrity. A society free of crime and strife begins with strong families. By fulfilling our roles as parents and stewards, we align with God's plan and contribute to building a harmonious and thriving world.

God's Promises And Parental Responsibilities

God's promises offer hope to parents seeking to instill faith in their children. Wise King Solomon emphasized the importance of guiding children to trust in God and His Word. Throughout the Scripture, parents are entrusted with the primary responsibility of teaching their children to understand, accept, and live by the principles of faith. A central aspect of this responsibility is passing down a spiritual heritage, ensuring that God's teachings and "secrets" are shared from one generation to the next.

To inspire faith in their children, parents must set a strong example through their actions and choices. A life rooted in faith serves as a powerful model for children, helping them adopt and sustain a faithful outlook. This demanding role often weighs heavily on a parent's heart, accompanied by the unending burden of ensuring their children's spiritual growth. God's promises, however, provide an unfailing source of strength for parents. These promises are reliable, enduring, and deeply reassuring for those tasked with guiding the next generation. King Solomon highlights the joy and pride that parents feel when their children grow to be honest, mature, wise, and obedient (Proverbs 23:24-25). Such qualities reflect the success of parental efforts in fostering a strong foundation of faith.

Parental responsibilities extend beyond spiritual education to living in the fear of the Lord and modeling a God-centered life. Theological training can play a vital role in equipping parents with the coping mechanisms and tools necessary to nurture their children's faith. God's promises encourage parents to trust Him for the wisdom, courage, and perseverance needed to fulfill their roles and continue shaping their children's spiritual journeys.

Essential Scriptures On Security And Family Guidance

Before diving into the specific promises of the Bible regarding security and family guidance, let's reflect on a few key scriptures that have been especially meaningful in our family. Discussing these verses at home can create opportunities for personal reflection and insights about God's unwavering commitment to your family's well-being. These promises not only strengthen our faith but also deepen our understanding of His care and guidance.

Matthew 10:29-31

> *"Are not two sparrows sold for a penny? Yet not one of them will fall to the ground outside your father's care. And even the very hairs of your head are all numbered. So don't be afraid; you are worth more than many sparrows."*

This scripture often comes up in our family prayers, especially when we ask for safety during travel. It reassures us that God's angels watch over us wherever we go and remain with our family members at home. This promise reminds us that God is intimately involved in every aspect of our lives, from the smallest details to the larger events.

Consider discussing these questions with your family: Do you believe that God arranges even the smallest details of your life? How does this make you feel about the more significant events you face? Encouraging your children to see God's involvement in their daily lives can help them develop trust in His protection and guidance through their work, worship, and relationships.

Deuteronomy 31:6

> *"Be strong and courageous. Do not be afraid or terrified because of them, for the Lord your God*

goes with you; He will never leave you nor forsake you."

This verse is a powerful reminder of God's presence and faithfulness. When discussing it with your children, you might explore who "them" refers to in the context of the Israelites' journey and how it applies to the challenges we face today.

Ask your children how they feel knowing that God will never leave or forsake them. What does this mean for the choices they make? This scripture encourages strength and courage, reminding us that God is always by our side, offering guidance and support no matter the situation.

By reflecting on these scriptures together, your family can grow in faith and draw closer to God, experiencing His promise of security and guidance in every aspect of life.

Promises Of Protection And Security

God has made countless promises to guide, guard, and protect His children. These promises are part of His covenant and serve as the foundation of the relationship between God and His people. Throughout the Bible, we see examples of God's faithfulness, where He fulfilled His promises by delivering His people from various troubles and dangers. One notable instance is His promise to Hagar. Facing scarcity and hardship, Hagar decided to leave Sarai's house and return to Egypt. In her vulnerable state as a single mother, God met her with encouragement, saying:

> *"You are now pregnant and you will give birth to a son. You shall name him Ishmael, for the Lord has heard of your misery. He will be a wild donkey of a man; his hand will be against everyone and everyone's hand against him, and he will live in hostility toward all his brothers."*

Security and safety are essential aspects of life that everyone desires. However, many factors can threaten these, leading to fear, uncertainty, and anxiety. Trusting in God and living in reverence to Him provides a strong foundation for both physical and spiritual protection. Conversely, a lack of faith often results in vulnerability and unease.

The Bible provides numerous examples of how God's promises brought strength and assurance to His people during critical moments. These stories remind us that true security is not derived from psychological strategies or motivational speeches but from the unwavering assurance of God's care. His promises instill courage, enabling His children to face life's challenges with confidence and faith.

God's care transforms lives from within, helping His followers overcome fear and anxiety. In a world filled with instability and uncertainty, His promises serve as a beacon of hope. They offer not only the courage to endure adversity but also the assurance of His constant presence and protection. Through His guidance and faithfulness, we can find peace and strength to navigate life's trials.

Physical Protection

There are times when we find ourselves in situations that seem impossible, and even those who are trained to respond, like police officers, are left in awe of how we were spared. But when we reflect on God's power and His promises, we realize that physical protection is something He has faithfully provided. As children of God, many of us can recall personal stories, incidents, and answers to prayer where God has intervened on our behalf, delivering us from harm. It's important to share these testimonies and remind ourselves of the ways God has protected us.

When we look at Scripture, we are amazed by the

countless ways God physically protected His people from danger. If we had the time, we could fill volumes with stories of God's intervention in times of peril. I encourage you to take God's promises to heart and apply them to your own life. Let His promises of refuge and protection be more than just temporary thoughts, let them guide you through times of physical danger. Prayer and memorizing scripture are essential tools in facing such challenges.

The first step is to pray and seek God's peace. This peace is not the absence of danger but the presence of God in the midst of it. Jesus experienced both danger and peace, and He offers us the same peace, even in the most terrifying circumstances. I think of a dear sister in Albania who, during a time of war, walked through the chaos with an unshakable peace. Let us also trust in God's protection, knowing that He is with us, no matter the danger we face.

www.ingramcontent.com/pod-product-compliance
Lightning Source LLC
Chambersburg PA
CBHW021621270326
41931CB00008B/801